BRITAIN WITH THE BRAKES OFF

BRITAIN WITH THE BRAKES OFF

by

H. F. R. CATHERWOOD

HODDER AND STOUGHTON

Printed in Great Britain for Hodder and Stoughton Ltd, St
Paul's House, Warwick Lane, London, E.C.4, by Cox &
Wyman Ltd, London, Reading and Fakenham

Preface

Although the majority of these speeches were made while I was a temporary civil servant, they do nevertheless reflect my own convictions and are not official apologia for the policies of the Government of the day. When I was asked to make a speech, I took a subject in which I was interested and which was in line with — or at least not at variance with — Government policy. The job of defending the whole Government platform belongs to members of the Government and their political supporters. The civil servant can afford to be selective, the politician cannot. The civil servant, if he does make speeches, is also somewhat more free to 'fly kites'. He does not carry his masters' weight of responsibility, and if his views turn out in the end to be outside the limits of Government policy, he has created no problems for himself or his masters. So although a speech-making civil servant is and will probably remain a rare bird and although he has to exercise more caution than the private citizen, he can nevertheless contribute something to the public debate. If he is in a policy-making department, he has the advantage of seeing all the papers on major policies and of taking part in some of the detailed argument. He has some idea of the problems and opportunities and the range of policies which might be adopted. The speeches he makes can help towards a better understanding of the choices which face the country.

Underlying these speeches is a common theme. It is that the spirit of gloom and cynicism which took hold of Britain in the early sixties is both unnecessary and damaging. I don't in the least deny that our economic performance could and should be better. I have advised on and taken part in some of the many television programmes on this theme. This was the burden of my job as Chief Industrial Adviser in the Department of Economic Affairs. But it is one thing to make constructive criticism in the belief that something can be done and another to make destructive criticism in the apparent belief that matters are beyond repair and all that is needed is to apportion the blame. That kind of criticism simply makes those who might put matters right retreat into their shells. As one doyen of financial journalism advised, 'Let's jam our hats on tight and prepare for squalls.' Economic advance depends on confidence — confidence that there are technical advances to be exploited, confidence that capital investment will be profitable, confidence that time and energy spent in developing our personal skills will be personally rewarding, confidence of labour in their management and of management in their labour that neither will restrict the economic advancement of the other, and confidence that change will lead not just to temporary disruption, but to a better way of life. The British people have not usually responded to bullying, but they have often responded to encouragement.

In the first chapter, I have tried to show some of the reasons why Britain, first and foremost an industrial nation, nevertheless tends to stand off from its industry, views it as something apart and does not see it as the very fabric of society, on which its whole welfare depends. I have argued that our social attitudes and our great national institutions have been geared to the *Pax Britannica* and to our imperial mission and that they must now be geared to the building of our industrial strength. In the next six chapters I have argued the case for bringing to industrial management all the expertise which we have deployed in building up the skill and standing of the older professions. I have pointed out that we are the founders of the very idea of professionalism and yet we have not developed it in industry where it matters most. I have also tried to argue a practical programme for the development of professionalism in industry. It is not easy, but I believe it can be done and my guess is that it will be done. In the next four chapters I have discussed the institutional changes now being made by Government and their likely impact on our economic growth. In the final chapter I have tried to show that Britain, whatever its critics may say, has a very strong basis for economic expansion.

Almost all the speeches were followed by periods of discussion, during which the views expressed came under some pretty brisk questioning. I have not modified them as a result, but I thought it might be helpful if I put in a few words at the beginning about the audience and their reactions. Since some of the speeches were made at a particular stage in the evolution of Government policy, I have also added a note to bring them up to date at the point of going to press and can only hope that they are not completely overtaken by events at the date of publication.

I am most grateful to Andrew Shonfield for all his advice and help and to my wife for her constructive criticism of the text. I would also like to thank Gus Mangraf for teaching me the rudimentary principles of the anti-trust legislation in the USA, two members of the Council of the Institute of Chartered Accountants for their advice on chapter seven (for which they are nevertheless not responsible!), to all who asked me to give the talks and those who later published them and not least to those who will find themselves, thinly disguised, as characters in the narrative.

Contents

To
ELIZABETH

The Next Five Years

This is an article published in The Times *on 3rd May 1966 and serves, I think, as a useful introduction, covering many of the subjects dealt with in the rest of the book.*

Five years ago the 1961 credit squeeze brought home to most people that there was something fundamentally wrong with the British economy and that something had to be done about it. Many people had, of course, felt this for far longer but I think it was about five years ago that opinion swung decisively, that most people felt the need of a change of course and of new initiatives.

The Government of the day responded with two major initiatives; it started to negotiate for membership of the European Economic Community and it set up the National Economic Development Council and made the first tentative steps in indicative planning. Of these the application to join the EEC was by far the most spectacular and its temporary failure, therefore, shook our morale and self-confidence.

When we had a further sterling crisis it was clear that indicative planning had to be more firmly supported by Government policies and by action in industry and in 1964 the new Government created the Department of Economic Affairs and the Ministry of Technology. It strongly supported the increase in the number of Economic Development Committees from nine, covering a quarter of industrial employment, to twenty, covering two-thirds of the private sector. It set up the National Board for Prices and Incomes and announced its intention of setting up an Industrial Reorganisation Corporation.

So far, so good. But will these new instruments do the trick? Have we really changed any of the fundamental policies?

If we have not, is a series of voluntary groups of men of goodwill sitting around the traditional green baize cloth really going to see us through? Or are they just a way of clouding the harsh unpleasant decisions we will one day have to make? These are fair questions.

In looking at them there is no need to be too gloomy. I see no reason to believe there is something fundamentally wrong with us as a people. Our trading account, taking visible and invisible trade together, has been in balance year in, year out. Our total overseas assets are substantially higher than our total overseas liabilities. We bear, however, a heavy burden of overseas responsibilities. Without these we would, no doubt, have a far easier time. But they are nothing to be ashamed of.

Although I do not, therefore, believe that it is primarily British industry's fault that our economy has been growing so slowly, I do not see any quick way out of our many burdens and I believe our future success is almost wholly in the hands of industry. I think that it will be hard work for industry to get the economy moving again, but I think we will succeed.

The first reason for my optimism is that I believe there is a great untapped reservoir of proven technical innovation. The introduction of new methods and new processes is often a tough job. But it pays management and men to get on with it, so that the work of the Ministry of Technology and of the EDCs is going with the interests of the market and not against them. What we need is to reduce the time-lag in putting proven new methods into common practice from say seven years to three years.

My second reason for optimism is that the new instruments of which I have most immediate experience, the EDCs, have, in spite of initial scepticism by many people, proved to be the hard-headed, practical and energetic bodies for which their advocates had hoped. The next five years will show whether these new instruments of collective self-help really do influence management and union decisions on a sufficient scale to make a material contribution to productivity and the balance of payments. If they go on as they have started, I have no doubt they will; but they face a lot of hard work.

My third reason for optimism is that while the new ministries and the plans they have produced can only be powerful instruments if they have general support, I do believe they are the real expression of a national will and do reflect a real change of direction in the course most people want Britain to take.

It is easy enough to belittle the changes which are made in the machinery of Government, to treat them as just another meaningless exercise, the reshuffling of the same old pack. My limited experience of that machinery is that this view is wrong. If powerful national figures are made responsible for doing something that the country wants and some of the ablest men in Government service are redeployed to help them, then a new centre of power has been brought into being in the national decision-making process and major national decisions will, from then on, have a different bias. Therefore, economic growth, I believe, will have higher priority in future.

The policy for productivity, prices and incomes has been in operation about a year. There is little doubt it has damped down the rise in the cost of living, but it is too early to say whether this has made wage increases lower than they might have been, still less to say whether the squeeze on margins has produced pressure within companies for higher productivity. It may be that many people are still hoping the whole unpleasant business will somehow go away. But there must come a time when even those who are most determined not to face the facts will realise that the policy is here to stay and that they must learn to live with it. At that point, I believe it will begin to make a much more visible effect than it has made in the first twelve months.

These will not be the only new instruments which we will need for Britain in the 1970s. While the EDCs are useful forums for reconciliation of the public interest in economic development with that of the individual company and union, I am sure there will be a major attempt to carry the dialogue down to the shop floor, through productivity committees. This will be a difficult exercise, but worth while because in much of British industry this is where the real decisions can be made.

I would not be surprised if companies who are already standard-bearers in economic performance and in the treatment of those who work for them and of their customers were given more formal recognition and I would expect company legislation in the next five years to give greatly increased weight to economic performance and social obligation.

I believe there will be some attempt to formalise a profession of management with primary entry through some technical skill such as engineering and with the secondary stage a more broadly based study of the science of management.

Lastly, I believe there will be strenuous efforts to put the mobility of the weekly paid employee on the same basis as the mobility of the salaried employee—who does not have to register as unemployed before he finds another job. I hope that in five years' time the vast majority of people will be able to find a new job while they are still employed in the old one and that the national and regional unemployment rates will be as irrelevant to the labour market as they are today for the market in managers.

No doubt there will be calls for more drastic policies—but drastic policies carry drastic risks, not least to personal freedom. No doubt also there will be some faint hearts who think the heavy slog of detailed work on industrial development not worth the effort. But do these people really think that a great country will tolerate a minute annual increase in national wealth and that all will go sedately on while other economies all around us are booming? In fact we have no option. We cannot stand still, we must go forward.

CHAPTER ONE

The Curious Attitude of the Educated Englishman to Industry

This talk was given in October 1965 to the Balance Group, a society of Cambridge undergraduates interested in careers in industry. It had a pretty enthusiastic response and the questioning was mainly on means and not on ends. The theme, that we had to turn our national talents from Empire to Industry and that we could do the one as well as we had done the other, seemed to be accepted.

I have put this speech at the beginning, because I believe this to be the *fundamental choice for the country and I am not at all sure that older generations have yet made it. Yet our future depends not only on our making the choice, but on our making it fast enough. It is not an easy course. Yesterday's commitments are a fact and we are a responsible nation. No one else wants the burden, least of all the Americans who have burdens enough already and who are ideologically opposed to the replacement of a* Pax Britannica *by a* Pax Americana. *Nor do we want a power vacuum. As a trading nation, we need the maximum of order and the minimum of hostile interference with trade around the world. So we are reluctant to cut our commitments unilaterally. But if our commitments are a strain on our financial resources now, could we really fulfil them if they were taken up in earnest? If we really want to turn from Empire to Industry, then we should take every opportunity to drop commitments and we should take the development of our industry with all the seriousness with which we took the development of our Empire. The fact is that for a mixture of reasons, some good and some bad, we have been paying some £600M to £700M* a year out of our national resources for the benefit of other countries' national resources and our investment in our own*

---

* Over the last year or so Aid has been running at about £200M, net currency costs of Defence are over £250M and net capital investment overseas at between £150M and £250M, the gross figure of overseas investment at much higher. It has been running at £300M to £400M). For detailed figures see Appendix 2.

economy has been less than that of all our major international rivals. We cannot go on with this handicap for ever. No one else except the United States carries this crippling burden and their national resources and reserves are much greater than ours. The post-war economic miracle is not that some countries at the receiving end have done well, but that Britain has kept it up for so long. What we are now distributing is not the surplus of past effort, but the seed-corn for our own future growth. To go on distributing that is not responsible generosity, but short-sighted folly.

Earlier this year, in its Annual Report, the Cambridge University Appointments Board reported: 'The number of Arts men taking appointments in industry and commerce again fell appreciably' (Annual Report for 1964).* When you set in the balance all those visits of personnel officers, all the glossy brochures, all the prestige advertising, the higher salaries offered by industry, the pension schemes and training schemes, the chances of promotion, the much greater security offered today and all those jobs spectacularly set out in the Sunday newspapers, this trend needs more than passing notice. Not only are the tangible rewards of industry greater, it is vital to the whole well-being of the country. Other nations which can at least feed themselves and are therefore not so dependent on industrial exports for their existence might well have other national priorities. We are a small island of 55 million people with a far higher income than most of the rest of the world and living entirely on our industrial skill. You would have thought, on the face of it, that this would be reflected in our social priorities and that industry would naturally have attracted all the best brains. How is it then that everyone seems to be making off in the opposite direction? And what, if anything, can be done about it?

I think that we have to go a little deeper than the marginal shift there has been in salaries. It is true that universities and the

* This may be an Oxbridge complaint. The report of the University Grants Committee for 'First Employment of University Graduates 1963–4' is much more encouraging, though both reports comment on the sharp increase in graduates going on to academic posts.

civil service have edged up a little on industry and the gap has narrowed. It is also true that academic and civil service holidays have always been a little longer. But we would hardly expect a slight lessening of the disadvantage in income to shift the preferences, or the odd week's holiday to change a man's choice of career. I think that there has been a strong underlying bias against an industrial career and it is this which must be examined rather than the fringe benefits. There was a time when Britain was quite frankly an industrial nation. We are almost the only nation in the world to have made an unaided economic breakthrough. We were the original economic miracle, the original 'operation bootstrap'. It was from the surpluses arising in Britain that the economic infrastructure of most other industrial nations was financed. British engineers built railways throughout the world. The City of London financed industrial development from Argentine to Imperial Russia, from China to the United States. British shipping dominated the seven seas. British trading companies were foremost in the world. In India, China, South America, West Africa and the West Indies, they bought our raw materials and sold our exports. All this economic growth was generated in these small islands. We had an empire of sorts, but until the mid-nineteenth century the major part of this was administered not by the British Government but by the East India Company.

It is hard to date the change in Britain's position exactly, but after a hundred years or more of solid industrial advance, the nation seems to have undergone a change of mood. If you look through old copies of *Punch* you will see certain snobbery creeping in in the late 1870s and the old down to earth quality is less evident. Plain honest John Bull appears less often and jokes are made at the expense of Sir Gorgeous Midas. Great deference is paid to titles; Mrs Ponsonby de Tompkyns and the Duchess of Stilton appear regularly and there is a good deal of mockery of those who do not know their way around in the fashionable world. This is, of course, the Victorian world our fathers remember and against which, to some extent, they revolted. But this is really not Victorian England so much as Imperial England. It seems to have come in with Disraeli in 1874 and it probably went out with Asquith and the Somme in 1916. Early Victorian Britain was a rather different sort of place. Samuel Smiles' 'Self-Help' was much more typical of its mood.

What, then, was the change of mood which came in with Disraeli and how does this affect us? My own belief is that whereas until then commerce and industry were our main interest and our Empire had been accumulated in a fit of absence of mind, after that date commerce and industry became secondary in the minds of our political and social leaders and the national will and energy were bent to the business of being a great imperial power. India, which had ceased to be in the preserve of the East India Company, became the Indian Empire and the old Queen became its first Empress. Colonial wars were fought in Africa and a whole new African empire was founded. The Suez Canal was bought and we became actively involved in the problems of the Near East. We began to rebuild our navy on a massive scale. At home, after the Trevelyan–Northcote reforms, we created a professional civil service and overseas there was a professional Indian civil service and later a colonial service. From having a loose association held together by commercial ties and some military protection, we began the direct administration from London of a vast and complex Empire, the largest the world has ever known.

This Empire had to have administrators who had not only to be trained technically but given a sense of mission and the will to go to the forsaken jungle and desert to rule alien people. The new private boarding schools to which the industrialists had begun to send their sons were the instrument ready to hand. Taken away from their parents and home environment, trained to live without women, to physical hardship and endurance, to put the team above the individual, tradition above intellect and loyalty above all else, they were the perfect training ground. To the older schools were added a whole host of brand new schools – with brand new traditions. There was Wellington which specialised in the Army and Imperial Service College specialising in the Indian civil service. In their wake came a whole host of minor schools and, in due course, since thirteen was rather too late for the break from home, came the private preparatory boarding schools which took boys as young as nine. What was of lasting importance in these schools was that they creamed off the boys who would have gone back into industry. Even this might not have mattered so much, because not everyone was needed for the service of state at home and abroad. It is said that India was actually run by no more than 2,000 expatriate administrative civil servants from Britain. But those who went back into industry had not been trained for it and the whole ethos of their schooling was against it. Inevitably they regarded it as second-best. I remember reading an exposition by H. W. Nevinson, who went to my old school, Shrewsbury before the turn of the century, of what did and did not constitute a gentleman. The industrialist did not. Inevitably, therefore, those who did go into business regarded it as second-best, treated it as second-best and, in the end, parts of it tended to become second-best. In countries not burdened with an empire, notably the United States, business was treated as the primary activity of the nation and great pride was taken in industrial achievements at the very time when we were turning our mind elsewhere. From the 1880s onwards our industrial primacy began to wane. Well, you may say, Disraeli has been dead a very long time, how does this affect us? It affects us because although certain parts of Victorianism came crashing about the ears of our fathers in the first world war, its imperial creation and institutions survived into our own time.* As late as 1943, the Government at Westminster ruled 750 million people, the largest empire the world has ever known. Even in 1960, no more than five years ago, the Empire alone numbered 100 million people, twice as big as the mother country. When I was at school in the war, the imperial ethos was still dominant. Last year the school issued a booklet showing what occupations we had all taken up. Of my contemporaries in my own house, I

---

* Some people argue that the survival of the Empire beyond the first world war was the result of a power-vacuum. Germany had been temporarily defeated. Russia was recovering from the effects of war and revolution and America, while disapproving of the Empire, was not prepared to do anything about it. The line-up at Suez showed how little we could do with two great powers against us. It is arguable that this is our real long-term position and is unlikely to be changed in the foreseeable future.

could only find one other in industry and he had come to us from a grammar school rather than a prep school and had left early, strongly allergic to the Public School Spirit. All the others seem to have gone into the civil service, the colonial service, the professions or farming (which because of its association with land counted as a gentlemanly occupation). Every generation over forty has, therefore, been subject to the force of the Imperial influence.

Secondly, the *Pax Britannica* was, by any standards, an overwhelming success and the savour of success lingers on until there is something quite as positive to put in its place or until it is discredited by association in the public mind with some awful catastrophe. We not only ran the largest empire the world has known, but on the whole we ruled with justice and when we went out with goodwill on all sides, drums beating and flags flying, we left behind the whole panoply of British Government and administration including a great many British administrators. I asked a Nigerian Chief the other day whether he thought that the British should have such a large force east of Suez. He said, 'Certainly you ought, how else could the area be defended?' So, although we have gone in law, we have not gone in spirit. Believe me, we have not. It must, of course, be extremely hard for those who have lived with the responsibilities of the *Pax Britannica* to believe that the great complex of forces on which it depended no longer exists. After all, we did fight for the freedom of the world twice in the twentieth century and we were overwhelmingly successful; for ten of the first forty-five years of the century we were at war. By and large, there has been order in our vast dominions. We are the only country to have beaten back Communist guerillas until they had to give up. Economically we have transformed the countries we ruled and have invested enormous amounts of our own savings in them. It is hard not to feel an obligation to go on with the work we have begun, even though we know that some day all these countries must stand on their own feet.

There have, of course, been a number of events which have demonstrated to those who were watching that all was not the same as it was before. On the military side there was Suez and on the economic side there was our loss of the sterling reserves in 1964. Both showed, in their respective spheres, that we were no longer capable of doing everything independently. Of our deficit of about £720M on balance of payments, military expenditure abroad accounted for £263M, official aid for £191M and gross overseas investment for £399M.* This accounts for more than the total deficit. It is significant, however, that the general mood was not to blame it on the wrong policy decisions but to blame it on industry for not being sufficiently competitive in exports. As a result the whole of foreign opinion is fixed on our improvement on current account (where we actually had a small surplus on visible and invisible trade) and not on the reversal of policies on capital account. Yet Britain already exports about 16% of its gross domestic product, half as much again as the Common Market's $10\frac{1}{2}$%† and the USA exports only $4\frac{1}{2}$%‡ When you try to find out why the import/export balance was the wrong way in 1964 you discover that the largest single factor was the curtailment of domestic investment in 1961 and 1962 because of the previous credit squeeze arising from the then balance of payments crisis. So that we are in a vicious circle of squeeze, low investment, low exports, high imports, payments deficit and more squeeze. You also discover that while we were pouring out our savings in overseas investment, our major competitors like Germany, Italy and Japan were investing their savings in their domestic industry and that there is, not surprisingly, the closest correlation in international comparisons between the annual rate of increase in domestic industrial investment and the annual rate of increase in exports.

There have also been political decisions which have begun to reflect the change. One was the decision to apply for entry to

* See Appendix 2. Even taking net overseas investment – and there is no reason to suppose that outflow from the UK greatly affects inflow to the UK – these figures still almost account for the total deficit.

† This excludes trade within the Common Market. Strictly speaking, Dutch goods sold in Belgium and Belgian goods sold in Holland are exports and all ECM countries have, of course, had soaring exports and imports as the tariffs came down inside the community. However, these sales within the common external tariff do not represent the same kind of export effort as our exports or America's.

‡ See Appendix A.

the Common Market, which no doubt would have provided the climatic change needed. The other is the Finance Act 1965, which changes the taxation incentive in favour of UK investment as against overseas investment. I do not think that, despite these evidences of change, we shall get our minds off the past until we have some positive role for the future and some positive blueprint for carrying out that role. What I suggest is that we must, once again, become the industrial leader of the world. It suits our skills, it suits our physical problems of population, geography and resources and it suits, as I think history has demonstrated, our national temperament.

However, to do this we need a lead as clear as our grandfathers had when Disraeli gave them his conception of Empire. We also need some fundamental and lasting changes in our national institutions, because no major changes in national direction can take place without changes in these institutions. If you leave the old institutions in place you will always get a strong bias towards the old policies. It was, and still is, their genius to carry out these policies, that is the world they really understand and it requires more effort and will-power than is normally available to steer them against their bias. But if you put a new collection of people together with new directives and policies and build the structure to serve the policies, there will usually be a very strong drive towards achieving those new policies. My limited experience of Government is that though political will is important it is not enough. Institutions matter a very great deal.

At Government level a good deal has been done. We have a Department of Economic Affairs with the positive job of encouraging overall economic development and not bound by particular responsibility for any one aspect of economic policy. We have the National Economic Development Council with members of Government, private and public industry, unions and independent members. We have Economic Development Councils for each major industry. We have a separate Ministry concerned at Government level with the application of technology. But none of these are enough to persuade our reluctant graduate or our reluctant schoolboy to enter industry, and unless more of our talent is attracted to industry all our other efforts will be relatively ineffective.

What then can be done? First of all, I believe that our basic educational system has to be altered so that it can do for industry what the private boarding school did for the Empire. Only an educationalist could say exactly what that alteration would entail. But I do not believe that a schoolboy's enthusiasm for industry can be stimulated by sending him for most of the year to the depths of rural England,* nor do I think that to confine him to intercourse with people of his own age and sex of one social class enables him to take his place naturally in the varied society of an industrial company. I should think that the ideal system would at least see that he was brought up among the people with whom he would eventually work. It might also be desirable to have a break between school and university for work in industry, say between seventeen and nineteen. This would enable the undergraduate to have a much better idea of the world he was going to work in and of the kind of speciality which appealed to him. Knowledge of practical problems would also be a considerable help and stimulus in subsequent academic study.

However, I do not think we can confine the changes which need to be made to Government and the educational system. Industry itself must become much more attractive to the schoolboy and undergraduate at the vital stage when they make up their minds about their careers. There are two possible paths, to some extent complementary, but to some extent opposed. One is the American path and that is the one which is the most generally advocated in industry at present. This is to make the rewards of success much greater, but to make sure that rewards are earned, the penalties of failure must also be greater. Industry must be more competitive and we all agree to that. But this means, say this school, that the ultimate personal rewards must be there for those who succeed and those who do not succeed must go to the wall far faster than they do at present. Taxes have to be lowered dramatically and merit has to be rewarded.

* We are making some progress. Eton College has just arranged some visits to companies in the Slough Trading Estate.

I argued this case on television in December 1960. I said that if the Chancellor halved the surtax on earned income, it would cost him less than 1% of his total revenue and he would more than make it up by the vast improvement in efficiency which would arise from the unleashing of all that talent at present discouraged by high rates of personal tax. Just do that, I said, and then stand back and watch the results. Four months later, in April 1961, the Chancellor did just that, but four years later the results are hard to see. There is nothing which fixes a thing in your mind so firmly as a public prediction which went wrong!

Rather than to try to adapt a product based on the American way of life, the other path is to adapt to British industry a truly indigenous British product. The British it was who invented the profession, professional standards and professional institutions. These are all well understood and well respected here, but, as we have noted, they have not been adapted to or adopted by industry. The reasons for this are, however, largely technical.

A profession presupposes a common body of knowledge and common standards based on common ethical problems. The techniques of industry, however, cover a vast range of knowledge and there has been little unified technical knowledge on which a profession could be based. The ethical problems too have been very different and industry itself varies from the one-man business to the vast industrial empire employing 100,000 people.

However, I do believe that the rise of management education and the standards of efficiency and integrity set by the leading companies now form the basis for a profession of management and the basis for public recognition of those companies which set themselves professional standards in their competence of management and in their relationship with their customers, employees and the public. I am sure that the attraction of the profession is that those who enter it know where they are. They are on charted seas where the rules of conduct are set out. To this extent they are independent of their immediate boss. Their position depends on their professional standing and not on the whims of one man's opinion. Their rewards are on an agreed scale and they do not have to go, cap in hand, asking their boss for a rise. Above all, they are not subject to arbitrary dismissal which, even with golden handshakes, can be the most catastrophic experience.

But even more important, they feel that there will be firm professional standards of performance which cannot be lowered by pressure to maximise short-term profits. Ask an undergraduate whether he would sooner be an architect or a builder and there is little doubt about his answer. Yet there should not be this demarcation. Both should be professionals, the one in design and the other in execution. The arbitrary distinction at present, the one being regarded as a profession and the other not, has caused the most lopsided and uneconomic structure in the building industry. I am sure too, that the old standing of the accountancy profession with its Royal Charter has resulted in accountants doing a great deal of work which might otherwise have been done by operational researchers or economists who do not have Royal Charters. I am also sure that those of us in industry who are members of professional bodies have far greater independence in the industrial jungle than those whose expertise has been gained in another way. When it comes to the pinch, you know (and your boss knows that you know) that you will risk your position in the company a great many times before you will risk your membership of your profession.

If a profession were formed which covered the whole field of industrial management, one has no doubt that the whole standing of the professional manager and the cause of professional management would be immeasurably strengthened. There are many technical problems still to be overcome but the National Economic Plan proposes that the Government should, as a start, consult with the various bodies concerned to see whether a further step can now be taken in the direction of professional management.

At company level I see no reason why those companies which now observe the highest standards should not have public recognition of the fact. There is, let us face it, a wide gap between the best in British industry, which compares with the best anywhere else in the world and the average or less than average. The trouble is that in the mind of the schoolboy and even the undergraduate they are all lumped together as business. The local tobacconist and the most backward and opinionated controlling director of a family business can call themselves a company director as well as the Chairman of Unilever. But it would be a real help in establishing industry as an attractive career for the best of the country's talent if those companies, large and small, where there was care in the training of managers, where there was a well-tried scheme of promotion, where there were high standards of management performance and proper joint consultation machinery with the unions, where there was above average export performance, good community relations and, above all, consistent value to customers, were to be specially and publicly recognised.

If I were attacking the ideas just put forward, I should no doubt say that it was very dangerous to give too much status to particular companies and to individual industrial managers. They had to be judged, in the end, by harsh economic realities and to dress them up in professional regalia was to give them a feeling of protection where none, in fact, existed. Did we want to go back to the protectionism of the guilds? Did I not know that professional bodies were the most obscurantist self-perpetuating oligarchies? What was needed was the cold clean wind of competition which made people perform because otherwise they would be out on their necks. What was *not* needed was the stuffiness of the institute council chamber. I'm sure I could make quite a tub-thumping speech. But I do not think that the arguments bear critical examination.

The professions are, in fact, highly competitive. Any barrister who has had to make his way will tell you that. When I was an articled clerk I sometimes used to have lunch in Grooms Coffee House just beside the Law Courts where impecunious barristers tried to borrow fivers and persuade each other that they were full of briefs. But the Bar Council sets standards to which they all conform and the profession provides the judges which make Britain's justice the envy of the world. I doubt if the 3,000 British architects would say that they were an uncompetitive profession and British civil engineers dominate the highly competitive market for international civil engineering projects.

Already we have the Restrictive Trade Practices Act, we have abolished resale price maintenance, there is a Monopolies Commission and what more can be done by law to promote industrial competition? I do not think that there is much further that we can go down that particular road and yet we do need a higher standard of performance from industry. The truth is that competition is only one of the means to the end of higher performance. It is an indirect means rather than a direct one and I believe that rather than going to the lengths of American Anti-Trust and all the vast paraphernalia of legislation, case-law and enforcement which that involves, we should do better to concentrate on improving the real standing of management. Part of the reason for such lack of competitiveness as exists is, I am convinced, because of a lack of professional understanding by some businessmen of market economics. If American business is competitive at two to three times our labour costs, it is because they have a professional understanding of the economics of scale and knowledge to translate this into pricing policies. Indeed, the Robinson–Patman Act is specifically aimed to prevent large companies from doing things to their commercial advantage which a lot of businessmen on this side of the Atlantic never seem even to have heard of.

One last point on competitiveness. A good many of the studies which have been carried out recently by the NEDC and Industry EDCs show that design rather than price is often the determining factor in international competition. Design is, in turn, based on professional skill. In consumer goods the Scandinavians have been particularly good at selling on design, and in engineering the Germans and Swiss made a specialty of good design. You just cannot, in the world today, afford to have the division which we have between the professions and business. Both must be thoroughly professional. Yet, for all its attraction, industrial management is a tougher career than academic life. The real problem today is to get things done through people despite the waywardness of human nature. The professions, as defined today, are technical jobs making, it is true, considerable demands on our brains, but because the end-product is usually advice rather than command they do not make such extensive demands on our personalities. It is one thing to design a new plant. It requires quite a different order of human strength of character to go and tell the men and women in the old one that you are closing down. It is one thing to programme a computer. It is quite another thing to persuade old Harry that he has spent forty years of his life doing the job the wrong way.

The critical problems today which will make or break us as a nation are the getting done in practice what is known to be feasible in theory. Theory is way ahead of practice and drawing further away every day. What we want is not more people to tell us from the security of the cloister what we ought to do and to criticise us for not doing it, but far more people who will go out and do it. Of course we need more academic research into industry. But what we need is the American kind of professor who spends at least five months of the year in the field advising clients on specific problems. The view there seems to be that if a professor of industrial management cannot earn his $400 a day from clients he is not fit to teach the university's students. It may be cosier sitting in your rooms in an ancient university giving a critical commentary on the faults of others, but it is not nearly so useful. The best blend is one of intellectual analysis and practical experience. Otherwise the analysis is likely to be constructed on a model which is based on all the available evidence minus some vital piece which did not happen to turn up in research, but which experience would have sensed and allowed for. We need fewer people on the sidelines and more in the field.

I am sure that we are on our way. There is an increasing interest in industrial management. There are the two new business schools. There is a group like your own in Cambridge and the summer school and new business school at Oxford as well as the course in the Engineering faculty here. To go back to *Punch*. There was a time not so long ago when *Punch* never mentioned industry. Now at least a quarter of its cartoons have an industrial setting and they have even had a joke about the Chief Industrial Adviser in the Department of Economic Affairs.

CHAPTER TWO

Scientific Management

The following talk was the James Dunn Lecture at Newcastle University, given in January 1966. There were no questions afterwards, but I had the feeling that the audience, which consisted both of academics and businessmen, were sympathetic with the theme, though in discussion over dinner afterwards, some of the businessmen evidently felt that scientific management was for the next generation!

There are two great problems facing business today. One is the development of systematic knowledge about industrial operations in a form which can usefully be passed on to others — the subject of this talk — and the other is the creation of institutions which will ensure that this knowledge is learnt, used and developed with all the skill and energy of which we are capable — which is the subject of chapter three.

I suppose that those of us who like to think of ourselves as scientific managers have a clearer idea of unscientific management than we have of the ideal scientific manager. Unscientific management is all round us. Typically, it tries to run the department, the shop, the plant, the business by hunch. Rather than work out a negotiating position, it prefers to 'play it by ear'. If competitors maintain prices, they are regarded as 'sound' if they cut them, they are 'cut-throat' and 'unsound'. Unscientific management does not introduce new plant, because the unions 'would never agree to work it'. It does not like cutting out old products which have had their day and clutter the production line because a few customers still buy them and 'they wouldn't like it if we refused to supply'. It hates delegation and has little idea how to control at several removes. It develops a mystique of the process, the market or the industry and refuses to believe that anyone who is not an initiate can possibly understand the mysteries or make any sensible remarks about them.

But if there is a caricature in our minds of the unscientific manager, we should recognise too that there is a caricature in their minds, and not in theirs alone, of the scientific manager. He is, in the caricature, usually young and he is full of ideas, but short on practice. He is certainly not to be let loose on the customer, on labour or any other outside group who matter to the business. If he disagrees with line management, he is to be overruled at once. He is regarded as an esoteric character, full of graphs, slide-rules, theories of psychological behaviour and other ideas which may be good in the text-books, but are quite useless on the shop-floor or in the rough and tumble of the market-place.

The trouble is that the more one side treats the other as a caricature and the less each allows his ideas to be modified in the cut and thrust of debate on actual situations, the more both will actually behave like caricatures. The world is littered with scientific managers disillusioned with the old hands and old hands disillusioned with so-called scientific managers. But both have a lot to learn from each other.

I started my business career here on Tyneside, when, in the spring of 1952, I was appointed Secretary and Chief Accountant of Laws Stores. I was an accountant, fresh from the City, short on practice, but full of ideas. My immediate boss was Grigor McClelland now principal of the Manchester Business School. He was fresh from Oxford and Henley Staff College. He was also full of ideas and had just taken over as Managing Director from Arthur McClelland, his father, who had built the business up. Arthur McClelland could distinguish a dozen different kinds of butter by taste alone. If a woman was walking out of a shop in Byker, having decided that 1/2d a pound was too dear, he would call out, 'It's only 7d a half', and back she would come and buy it. He knew his customers and he knew his wares. He would have been less than human to wonder just what scientific management was going to do to Laws Stores. Grigor was determined that the basis of scientific management was to get at the facts and before I arrived, a Powers-Samas punched card machine had been ordered. This was the equivalent in those days of a computer and had not previously been heard of in Hawks Road, Gateshead. So we were to go straight from the horse and buggy to the jet. I was sent off to London on a course and in due time the machine arrived with boxes and boxes of cards. From that day to this, I have never forgotten the lesson that the output of a complicated piece of hardware is no better than its input and that the input depends on people. Arthur McClelland's first strength was that he let us do it at all. His second was that when this expensive piece of equipment started to churn out all the wrong answers, he had the patience and courage to let us plough on. In the end the machine imposed its logic on the control system and that in turn became both firmer and better. In due course the whole business was better off and by that time both the older and younger generation had developed a strong regard for the expertise of the other. But the credit really goes to the older generation for having allowed this and other experiments in scientific management.

What then is the particular expertise of scientific management? What is it that the business schools should try to teach? And is there anything which cannot and should not be taught?

Science, as I understand it, is systematised knowledge, especially knowledge about the world we live in. And the Scientific Method, as I understand it, assumes that the ground rules, when you have discovered them, will remain constant, so that you have only to diagnose the situation and discover the particular set of rules which apply to it, in order to know what action is needed to produce a particular reaction. No one suggests that management is an exact science like chemistry or physics. First of all the experts are not agreed on the laws which govern economics and secondly, human beings are much more unpredictable than matter. What the scientific manager would say, however, is that even if you cannot teach men bravery, you must still train them in the science of war, if you cannot teach men to be leaders, you must still have a Sandhurst to train them to be officers. Our children may not be Mozarts, but we can still teach them to play the piano and to develop such sense of tone and rhythm as they have. There is a body of knowledge about industrial management which can and should be taught and we shall be the richer for that knowledge and the poorer without it.

I suggest that the first objective of scientific management is that the manager should know all the options which are open to him in any given situation. Too often there seems to a management group to be only one thing to be done and that is usually unpleasant! This is hardly surprising. Most of us are brought up in one industry. A lot of us stay with the same company most of our working lives. What we learn by experience is therefore governed by the pattern of our industry or even by the pattern of one company for a fairly limited time in its history. It is, however, most unlikely that the particular pattern of which we have first-hand experience will ever again be repeated. The conditions which created it have almost certainly gone for good. Even in one industry, not even jobbing backwards, it is enough to know what happened; if the experience is not to mislead us, we must also know why it happened. But we cannot know why unless we have some theoretical knowledge, some conceptual model against which we can test the facts. Some people do, of course, get by without really knowing the whys and wherefores of what goes on around them. But they would make much better decisions if they did know. It is a constant source of surprise to me to find out how little people know of the ways in which others have tackled problems which are very similar to their own and how narrowly they see the range of options open to them. Perhaps this is because each company has to argue out its strategy in secret — if it argues it out at all — and there is no forum in which all the assumptions of the management group can be questioned and a range of possible alternatives put. It is therefore vital that the management of each company should have a range of knowledge much wider than that which is likely to arise within their own company and from their own experience.

The danger of only seeing one way out of a situation is that it can lead to an unbalanced and even obsessive attitude to the chosen solution even when it is quite clear that it is failing. It is not easy to take industrial examples because of the secrecy which shrouds corporate decisions. But there are endless military examples where inadequately trained generals could only see one way out. There were two possible solutions to the military stalemate on the Western front in the first world war. One was the massive use of tanks, but these were frittered away prematurely in small numbers in the indecisive Battle of Cambrai. The other was to try to open a Balkan front and this came to pieces through lack of support at Gallipoli. The orthodox military answer was frontal attack and the generals persisted at the Somme and Passchendaele even though it was immediately clear that they could not possibly reach their objectives. We can be thankful that in the next war our military leadership was better trained.

In industrial affairs the options seem perhaps most limited in the field of labour relations. Too often a firm considers that it has no option but to face a disastrous strike or to concede whatever demands are made. Time and again responsible union leaders find themselves outbid by shop-floor activists because management have given way under pressure. Yet there are times, such as the famous Rootes strike in the early 1960s when a management has taken a long look forward, decided that enough is enough and gone for the other option. Nor is this always disastrous. I remember facing the threat of a strike in an enormous plant operating by continuous process where a strike could quite easily wipe out the whole year's profits. However we decided that the plant, which was fairly new, was likely to be in operation for a very long time, that if it became evident that the management would not risk a strike our negotiating position for year after year would be worthless. We thought that it was desirable to establish early on that if having negotiated a reasonable deal in good faith, we were then faced with a walk-out in breach of agreement, we would be perfectly prepared to face a strike. Instructions were given to the plant management to put into effect the agreed close-down procedures. But the men came in to protest. The shop stewards had assured them, they said, that there would be no strike because the management could not afford it. The management said that nevertheless the shop stewards had given official notice and

35

unless they held a further meeting and voted to the contrary, the plant would continue to be closed by the agreed procedure. In next to no time the meeting was held, the vote reversed and with only hours to go, the plant stayed open.

I should like to take another problem of labour relations, the closing down of old facilities. Too often management boggle at this problem. They fear that it will produce strikes in their remaining plants, that it will be impossible to maintain delivery times and product quality with a declining and unbalanced labour force. There is also, in most of us, an emotional dislike of admitting that a job which has engaged men's skill and perhaps their whole working lives is no longer relevant to the needs of the day. Since this kind of decision only comes to a company once in a while, it normally has no experience in carrying out a closure; but a closure is nevertheless a highly skilled operation. Indeed the company probably has no experience even in sensing that the moment has arrived when the operation cannot be delayed without serious effects on the business. The old inherited expertise within the company cannot help. The skills which are needed must come from outside the company's experience. They can only come therefore from a study of first principles and from finding out what other people have done in similar circumstances. This is the stuff of scientific management.

The closure of an old plant is an unpleasant experience and the managing director of a company should take the personal responsibility of going to the plant to announce it so that any spanners which happen to be flying round hit the right target. I have only had one experience of doing this kind of thing and it may offer some consolation to those who may face it in the future, to know that in our case the union's final demand was that there should be a series of farewell dinners as each group was laid off and that the directors should attend them and present the redundancy cheques in person. I may also add that that particular plant maintained its quality and delivery dates until the last machine closed down. That this particular closure was successful was due entirely to the professional competence of the plant management and the company's industrial engineers and personnel management, who brought to it all the knowledge and experience then available on plant closures and set a new standard for terms of compensation. For those interested all this has been set out in *The Milton Story* by Alan Fox.

Knowledge of all the available options is most unlikely to come by natural process from inside the company. Why should it? In no other walk of life is any one group of men expected to have all the answers. No one school, however distinguished, supposes that it can learn nothing from outside about teaching. No one hospital, however renowned its medical school, thinks that it has all the brains in the world of medicine. There should be no army staff college worth its salt which does not pay attention to the body of military knowledge throughout the world. Of course, the teacher, the doctor and the soldier have, in the end, to deal with human beings and with their peculiarities and limitations, but that makes them the more and not the less anxious to have all the knowledge available and to discuss with each other their experience of its practical application.

Looked at from the outside, some companies appear enormous. They employ perhaps as much as 50,000 people and tens of millions pounds' worth of capital. It is hard, from the outside, to believe that they do not have all the skills they need within the company. Yet when you look at the whole British industry, a company, even of this size, employs only a fraction of 1% of the labour force and contributes only a fraction of 1% to the gross national product. And when you talk to chairmen and managing directors, all of them say that they are short of the management skills they need. If even the largest companies are short of management skills and the knowledge that goes with them, the need of smaller companies must be greater. Yet it is so often the largest companies which see the need when the smaller ones do not. The other day I visited the president of one of the largest American motor manufacturers. As soon as we had got through our rather tough agenda, he turned at once to the subject of scientific management. By any standards it was a company with enormous resources and extremely successful, but nevertheless it insisted on having available to it the best and latest tools of scientific management, and a steady stream of the best graduates from the top American business schools. It was not sufficient to rely on the experience it gained within its own operations, wide ranging and successful though they were.

I imagine that the reason for the resistance to scientific management is not so much that people do not want to know what there is to be known, but that they do not see how they can possibly make it relevant to their own business. They do not mind knowing all the available options so long as they do not have to know twelve thousand. All they ask for is more than one. If they are faced in their in-tray with two or three practical decisions and two or three management publications, the chances are that it will seem more relevant to make the practical decisions and to send the management publications to the personnel officer. However, the fact that the manager of today sees the problem in those terms is simply a reflection of our inadequate means for teaching scientific management. The difference between our harassed manager who does not read management publications and the equally harassed general practitioner who does read the *British Medical Journal* or the *Lancet* is that the latter has a formal framework of knowledge to which he is constantly relating his practical experience and the *BMJ* and the *Lancet* help him to do this. It is a rare manager who has such a formal framework. The GP has had a six-year stint at university and teaching hospital and maybe much of what he has learned he will never use. The specialist has had two or three years in addition. But though they never use much of the detailed information, they know where to find it when they need it and they have been taught the methods of diagnosis which enable them to relate what they find in practice to what they have learned in theory. None of this can give a doctor human sympathy and understanding if he does not have it. Nor can it give the judgement of human beings as a whole which a good doctor needs. These are developed by practice. But this is no reason for opposing the training of doctors in sound medicine. The same arguments apply, and not too differently, to management. The case for business schools is just as strong as the case for medical schools and if you think that medicine is a more exact science than business, all you need is a few doctors in your circle of friends and relations!

Let us assume that we are no longer bewildered by the variety of knowledge about management, that we know our way about it and that we want to use it in our own business and on our own problems. Does scientific management tell us how to set about it, or is this all still a matter of human judgement? Well it would be an odd teacher of medicine which did not tell his pupils how to diagnose and prescribe. It would be an odd military textbook which had nothing about the application of tactics and strategy. The trouble with so many well-meaning attempts at putting the principles of good management into practice is that people do not know where to begin, and do not realise that methods of application have to be taught too, and become disillusioned with what they think is scientific management, because they have never given it a chance.

Scientific management begins, as does medicine, with diagnosis. It must deal with underlying causes, not with symptoms. The symptom may be a wildcat strike, but the diagnosis may indicate an entirely misguided system of labour relations. The symptom may be an unexpected increase in stock and debtors, but the diagnosis may be heavy losses which the current accounting system does not bring to light. The symptom may be the loss in succession of a number of promising young managers, all earning high salaries, but the diagnosis may be an outdated system of organisational control. The symptom may be a declining market share, but with business apparently coming in as usual. The diagnosis may reveal that competition has started selective price-cutting to gain a foothold with each of the company's major accounts.

Unscientific management, confronted with these symptoms, will try to deal with them directly and will not succeed. They will no doubt blame the wildcats on the Communists, issue instructions for an all-round slashing of stock and debtors, raise managerial salaries to giddy heights and start a major sales promotional drive. None of these actions will have the slightest effect and will no doubt confirm unscientific managers with the view that since they cannot understand the problem, no one else is likely to do so either, that what is necessary is not a lot of ballyhoo about scientific management, but courage to withstand the shocks and the will-power to press on regardless.

The first rule of diagnosis is to ask a lot of questions. This, of course, runs straight into one of the first rules of unscientific management which is that your job is a mystery which no one else should be allowed to discover. If anyone asks questions about it, this should be treated as a Vote of No Confidence to which an injured and dignified silence is the only answer. There will also be references no doubt to the fact that certain Higher Authorities would not like it. However, since the scientific manager is unworthy of the name who does not know his tactics as well as his strategy, he will no doubt already have squared the Higher Authorities.

The more experience I have of other walks of life, the odder I find the absence of critical questioning in business life. We may think we ask critical questions, but we do not. The occasions when we do are so rare that the chap on the wrong end of the cross-fire usually expects to get his cards the next day and starts looking for another job just in case. On the other hand the civil servant, whose job and rank are perfectly secure, takes these things in his stride. I shall never forget my first traumatic experience of civil service cross-questioning when I attended an inter-departmental civil service committee in my first week to explain a proposed DEA policy to twenty or so Permanent Secretaries. Every assumption I had ever made — and a good many I hadn't, but might have — were taken apart, turned inside out and put back together again (I am glad to say that the DEA policy nevertheless survived). We could do with a good deal more of that in business. But, since the tenure of office is a good deal less secure in business than in other walks of life, we need to involve those responsible *with* us in the examination of the facts so that it is an examination of the facts and not of them. Even if something is going to be discovered about the people involved, it should arise from mutually agreed facts and not from a bandying round of opinion on personalities.

Much of the skill in getting hard evidence arises from knowing the right questions and these in turn arise from the knowledge which a scientific manager will possess, from his general reading and from case-studies, of businesses and industries other than his own. It should also arise from the kind of analytical mind that any scientific training should give. The questioner will be testing to see whether the situation fits any known model. So far as it does, the model may provide the answers. Usually it fits imperfectly and the skill lies in finding the differences and in deciding how this alters the solutions. There are, for instance, many models of price competition. The variables include the number of buyers, the number of sellers, the spare capacity in the industry, the degree of tariff protection, whether the industry is labour or capital intensive, the degree of substitutability in the products, the annual rate of increase of the total market, the opportunities in export markets and many other variables. Faced with price competition, we need to know all the answers to these and a good many other questions. Then we can construct our model—an oligopolistic market with a weak price leader, low tariffs, high capitalisation, high substitutability, lots of spare capacity, gradual exclusion from traditional export markets. Where else, we then ask, have these conditions ruled and what strategy brought which company out on top? We may try to get two or three models so that the peculiar oddity of one situation gets ruled out. Then from this we build our own initial strategy, modifying it by experience as we go along.

Internal problems are often more difficult to analyse, because the attitude of management is more subjective. I remember once looking at the unprofitability of a product which I was told *should* be making a profit. However, every variant of the product was making a loss and dragging down the profitability of the company. It seemed to be a complete mystery. Then I decided to try to get back to the point at which the product had made a profit and find out what had gone wrong since. One variant had hit the jackpot in 1951, another in 1954, but apart from these years and going right back to the war I found that the product had always made a loss. Even taking these two profitable years into consideration it had made a stiff overall loss. The 1951 and 1954 products turned out to have been sold at an exceptionally good price because someone in both cases wanted a lot in a hurry and not because of more efficient production. I came to the conclusion that the company did not have—and never had had—the real skill needed to make the product, but because it was the most technically advanced in the whole range, it could not bring itself to admit it. To justify its expectations it made the two freak years the norm to which it always hoped to return. However, having once admitted that it had not the skills needed, it set about finding the people who had these skills and in a short time had an extremely profitable product.

Sometimes the internal problem does not arise from a single product, but from a whole plant. If you think that the performance of a plant is poor, you must first of all have some sort of specification of optimum performance against which to measure it. The manager without access to any experience outside his own company does not find this nearly so easy as the manager with some basic training in an aspect of scientific management like industrial engineering. The one is only sometimes conscious of the yardstick, the other almost always. But once you have the yardstick, you begin to know the kind of questions you should ask. What is the ratio of maintenance men to line production men? What is the ratio of planned to unplanned maintenance? What is the cost of down-time for unplanned maintenance? How much consequential idle time results from unplanned maintenance? If there is a breakdown can the crews be switched from machine to machine? Does there seem to be any correlation between the age of machines and their down-time? What are the bottleneck machines? What are their total weekly hours of productive running? And so we might go on until some pattern emerged of what really went on in that plant, not excluding what happened on the night shift. Needless to say no scientific manager will think that he can get all the answers from an office in London. It is not always what he actually sees, but what people tell him when he walks round which it would not occur to them to tell him if he didn't happen to be there.

Having asked all the questions, analysed the answers, compared them with the models based on a wide range of practical experience, and having finally decided what needs to be done, scientific management faces its greatest test. Can it make any contribution whatever to getting things done, or must it remain a back-room, slide-rule kind of occupation, condemned always to advise, but never to do; on tap, but never on top?

We must admit that in getting people to do things, a strong element of personality comes in. We must also admit that science is based on predictable knowledge, on knowledge of what happens to elements under the same influences and conditions. But human nature can be unpredictable and at times even perverse. It is influenced not only by reason but also by emotion. In a face to face encounter it is influenced by irrational likes and dislikes. What chance has cold reason in face of inflamed prejudice? Faced with these conditions we instinctively reach for the tough manager, the fast-talking salesman and not the white-coated scientist.

We must also admit that some attempts to deal with the problem by reducing human beings to the level of predictable machines leave us pretty cold. Having once been through a personality test myself, I should be most reluctant to be responsible for putting anyone else through one. I commend to you William Whyte's *Organisation Man*, especially the bits on how to cheat the personality tester! I do not deny that these tests can pick up a schizophrenic, nor that some of them can tell you something about a man's personality. But they are dangerous in giving a spurious appearance of finality and accuracy, and they are, I think, wrong in requiring a man to lay bare more of his soul to a public company than he would do to his closest friend.

Having said all this, I still think that scientific management has a great deal to offer in the field of getting things done. The fact is that there are simply not enough great and dynamic personalities to go round and we have to make do with the chaps we have. It does not require a genius of a sales director to descend into the arena and make a sale himself. What does require genius is to produce the kind of sales force which makes this unnecessary. It has often been said that the best in British management is as good as the best anywhere else in the world.

Where we tend to be behind is that we are not so good at making an average middle manager into a top performer. This is where I believe that the Americans have the edge. Most of us have some sort of leadership and powers of persuasion which are capable of development. And most of us have some capacity to pick up the experience and ideas of others on persuasion and leadership and to try them out ourselves. Give a man the chance and it is surprising how well he will do.

People are not completely unpredictable, and it is possible to form some general rules of conduct which will see us through with most of the people most of the time. (If you do not believe me I commend to you the Book of Proverbs of Solomon which makes as good sense to us today as it did to the ancient Jews.) Most people prefer a request rather than an order, like to be given a reason, will do most things in reason if they are consulted first and will give respect to those who give respect to them. Although life is full of emotion, it is almost always right to meet emotion with reason and almost always wrong to meet emotion with emotion. There is no magic in leadership. It is mostly a matter of persuading people that you know what you are about, that you are considerate for their interests and that what you want them to do is therefore sensible and in their interests. I don't deny that there is a lunatic fringe, but the way to deal with it is to get the body of sensible people on your side and they will usually look after it for you. Above all what is needed is respect for other people as human beings. With all his scientific training, someone who despises his fellows can never do a good job as a manager. People are quick to spot arrogance and they will usually try to lay it low. But I have found in practice that it is not usually the scientific, but the unscientific manager who is arrogant, who shouts at people, who will not listen to their case and who feels that he must assert himself. At least the scientific manager should have had the right principles drummed into him at some time and, all else being equal, is more likely to go right and less likely by his attitude to bring down disaster.

One rule, propounded by that doyen of scientific management Peter Drucker, which I have found especially helpful in managing the work of managers is that one should always build on strength and never on weakness. If a man cannot do a job, one should, of course, find out why. But it is much more important to find out what he can do than what he cannot. There is hardly anyone who is utterly without ability to make a contribution of some kind in a management team. If he cannot do the job, do not respond by putting all kinds of checks and restrictions on him to try to minimise his mistakes. It is not fair to those under him or those responsible for him and above all it is not fair to the man himself. If the job does not matter all that much and there is no one else to do it, let him have a go without breathing down his neck. It may be that this will bring out unexpected strengths. But if the job is too important to take risks, then go to some trouble to find him a job he really can do well. It is what he *can* do and not what he cannot do that matters to the company and it is the feeling on the part of every single manager that he is doing a job that matters that makes for the *esprit de corps* of a really good management team.

Although scientific management has its role to play in persuading other people to do things inside the company, it is in the role of external persuasion that it makes the decisive contribution. Who would have an unskilled negotiator by his side when he could have a skilled one? One of my present colleagues in the DEA is an unsurpassed negotiator. I was once told by someone who had had his help in an important international negotiation that his genius lay in his ability to see several moves ahead. He would point out to his side's spokesman that in ten minutes the Italians, although they hadn't thought of it yet, would make such and such a point and that his reply should be so and so, and that would be exactly what would happen. But this ability does not come from second sight. It comes from knowing as well as anyone else round the table, the underlying factors in the discussion, from an understanding of the real interests of the other parties as well as their fears and prejudices, from a thorough understanding of the interests you represent yourself, the points you can concede without damage and the point at which you are prepared to see the whole deal fall to the ground rather than make a single extra concession.

This latter point is a very hard one to judge before you are actually at the crunch. It is also very hard, unless you are able to judge it ahead of time to make the other side believe that you are not just making another negotiating point. Tough negotiations cannot be played by ear. You have to have the moves and counter-moves scientifically mapped out ahead. I had once to inform the trade commissioners of another country that our side had come to the end of the road. I had an immediate invitation to go there to discuss the matter with them. But we really *had* come to the end of the road. There were no concessions to be made. So I stayed where I was. Had I gone, they would have reasoned that there must be concessions to be made on our side and would have held out for them. As it was it was clear that there were none and after a hair-raising wait while both sides tested the other's nerves, we had a message from their embassy to say that our terms had been accepted.

Iron nerves and a poker face may be a negotiator's stock in trade, but what is necessary above all else is that he should know his business, and his business includes the business of the other party to the deal. The salesman who really succeeds is not the back-slapping hearty of the golf-club bar, but the man who can fit his sale into the context of the customer's business in a way that makes sense to the customer. You can still meet the salesman with that 'get out and sell' cartoon on his desk. But behind him, beside him or, more likely today, above him is the marketing manager, who thinks out his strategy and the tactics without which the old-time salesman with all his gifts could no longer compete.

I have tried to show the kind of ground which scientific management should cover and the kind of help it should give. Business still requires judgement both of situations and of people, it still needs nerve and courage, integrity and reliability. But scientific management is not opposed to these qualities. It aims to develop them and having done that, to work with them.

CHAPTER THREE

Professional Management

This was a talk to the British Institute of Management in Rochester in October 1965. Theoretical knowledge is growing much faster than its practical application. Our standard of living now depends on our doing in practice what we know can be done in theory. If we were to do this, we could improve our industrial productivity at two or three times the present rate—perhaps much more. The second industrial revolution has arrived in theory, but not in practice. In other fields the instrument of advance has been the development of a profession. Can we have this for industrial management? Because of the complexity of industry and its size, this has not so far been possible. But I believe we can and should have a profession of industrial management.

The audience was very mixed, consisting not only of the Mayor and one or two Aldermen of Rochester, but also of naval officers from the nearby Royal Naval Dockyard at Chatham and army officers from a nearby military establishment. I was very sorry to have to inflict on them, especially on the civic dignitaries, a rather advanced argument on a difficult subject. The atmosphere of the Assembly Rooms, Rochester, with their gilt, chandeliers and nets in the ceiling for holding balloons on festive occasions, was, after a good dinner, not the most conducive for serious professional argument. However, the members of the Institute responded well and the talk was followed by some very constructive questioning. These centred on the adequacy or otherwise of the market economy to look after the general good and I was taken up, though none too confidently, on my implicit questioning of the conventional wisdom that the market economy is entirely adequate to the needs of today.

We are told today that what we need in British management is less amateurism and more professionalism—and, indeed, that is true. But too seldom is there time for us to pause and ask ourselves what we really mean by professionalism. Is it a matter of status? Is it a matter of training? Is it putting full-time executives on the board instead of part-timers from some other walk of life? Or is it something more than all these? I believe, myself, that it is something much more coherent and specific than all these general ideas. A profession is a body of people with a common skill, devoted both to the practice and the development of that skill, with firm rules of entry and of conduct drawn up to protect the public and with equally firm sanctions should those rules be broken. It is not just some worthy do-goodism, generally applauded but relatively ineffective. It is a specific and effective instrument devoted to a specific and effective purpose.

The professions as we know them are very much a British invention. Yet, despite the fact that we are essentially an industrial and trading nation, we have no profession of management. We need, therefore, to ask ourselves why this is, whether it matters and, if it does matter what can be done about it.

It seems to me that there are a number of quite different reasons for the absence of any profession of management. First of all, a great many managers are already members of other professions and have no need for professional standing because they have it already. If you look at the qualifications of company directors you will find that a great many board members are also engineers, chartered accountants, lawyers, and so on. Some have come in from the civil service, the colonial service and the armed forces and have, although not members of a profession in the formal sense, brought their professional standing with them. They have built up a reputation in those other spheres which they are not going to compromise.

Secondly, there has not, until now, been a coherent body of knowledge on management. There has been knowledge of particular skills, chemistry, electrical engineering, accountancy, economics, all backed up by a growing body of academic knowledge, but no agreed body of knowledge on the bringing together and marketing of those skills by a corporate management.

Thirdly, the professions were built up on the ideal of individual service and did not find a natural place in a complex corporate hierarchy. When you were paid by the client whom it was your professional duty to serve, there was no conflict, but when you were paid by the company, the presumption was that your first duty was to serve the company. This raised possible conflicts of interest. Finally, and not least important, there was a tendency on the part of the educated Englishman to go into a recognised profession instead of business, so that those who were in business were those who were least anxious about professional standing. Had they been anxious about it, they would have chosen the professions instead. The business community tended, therefore, for all those reasons to remain outside the professional field.

It can, of course, be argued that this does not matter, that business and the professions are essentially different. The giving of professional standing to management is not what most people would believe was most necessary in putting Britain on its feet again. I am not sure, however, that most people would be right. It is vital for our whole future that industry has its fair share of the skill and intelligence of the country and it is vital that what skill and intelligence it has shall be properly used. But the proportion of undergraduates planning to go into industry is still lower than one might expect. The reason cannot be money —industry still offers both immediately and ultimately far higher financial rewards. It seems to depend more on the greater independence, security and personal standing given by academic life and the professions, and the greater opportunity they give to develop the skills which undergraduates have studied to acquire. Where they do choose business, it seems sometimes to be just for the money, which gives them the chance of developing their other interests outside the business or even because they do not think they will make the grade elsewhere. Even those who do go into industry are too often disillusioned and either return to other walks of life or emigrate. This is not a situation which can be tolerated for long by a nation which relies for its survival on its industrial success.

In the second place, the instruments which we have to hand for improving our industrial performance as a country really need a strong profession of industrial management to back them up. At present, we rely on the forces of competition, on co-operative activity through bodies such as NEDC and the Industry EDCs (the big and little Neddies) and through fiscal and monetary policies. All these instruments, however, can do no more than provide the background against which the active and creative decisions are taken within the companies themselves. Exhortation and persuasion can only go so far. The power of Government in a democracy (or perhaps, indeed, in any country) is limited. It can only provide the framework and point the way. It depends for action entirely on industrial management itself. If management does not act, nothing will happen. We must improve our standard of management for national survival.

Thirdly, the controlling power of the public shareholder in the big company has gone and gone for good. He has only one right left, the right to abdicate. This has left a vacuum which a democratic society will one day want to fill. It would be legally possible to reimpose shareholder control, but I do not believe that political support could now be found for such legislation. Without shareholder control there are only two alternative ways of having any form of rationalisation of the power of industrial management.

One is public ownership and the other is the creation of self-imposed professional standards. I imagine that the majority of industrial managers would prefer the latter. Indeed, if you read some of the early socialists, you will find that they regarded public ownership as a means to this end. But I doubt whether industrial managers would believe that it is the only means by which to obtain responsible professional management.

It can be argued that the Americans, whose professionalism in management is beyond dispute, do not have a formal professional institution. In the sense that they have no disciplinary body this is certainly true. But they do have a very strong academic discipline in management, backed by the great business schools like Stanford, MIT and Harvard and dozens of less well-known, but almost equally good business schools all across the country. They also have two sanctions which may be more effective than desirable, an unemployment rate three times our own and more penal legislation on competition. Finally, their need is not so great as ours. They have a comfortable trade surplus while only exporting 4½% of their gross domestic product, while we have to export 16% to achieve a surplus on visible and invisible trade. This calls for a much closer identification of individual and national interests than the Americans will ever need.

But it is when you look inside today's corporation that you find the most compelling case for a full-blooded professional institution of management. Companies are undoubtedly going to grow in size. The National Economic Plan recognises that international competition must dictate the size of the economic unit and, this being so, the unit can only get larger. The scale needed for the most economic capital equipment giving the longest runs, the scale needed to treat the world and not just the UK as a market, the scale needed for research and more especially for development (which cannot be bought out) all dictate increasing size. But with size come problems. If you do not overcome those problems you get William Whyte's organisation man and the world of C. Wright Mills' *White Collar* not to mention Parkinson's Law, which though not in the same class of sociological research has enough truth in it to warrant mention. But if we are to have huge corporations, there must be some standards by which the human beings who compose them behave towards each other and towards the world outside, some known standard to which those who run the corporation can refer, otherwise the corporation becomes arbitrary in its behaviour and a democracy cannot tolerate arbitrary behaviour in powerful economic centres worth tens of millions of pounds and employing tens of thousands of people. It is possible for them either to set their own standards or to have an objective standard to which they and those who work for them can refer. An employing body like the army or civil service in which men will spend the whole of their working lives, can and must set its own standards. However, in industry it is most desirable that there should be mobility of managers between company and company and, therefore, there should be some uniformity of standards between companies. It is also desirable that in a large and powerful institution able to dismiss men from its service, to make or break their reputation and to give most generous financial rewards, managers should have some loyalty to institutional standards outside the power of the particular organisation which, for the moment, happens to pay their salary. Of course, many companies do have the highest standards, high enough to be our guides, but it is hard for the outsider to know which do and which do not.

There remain the practical problems of having a profession based on so many different skills and covering the whole of the vast complex of industrial and commercial life. But given the need, and the need is indeed compelling, the way round these problems will, I am sure, be found.

First, there is the question of the objective assessment of the skills which a man must have before he can be recognised as a professional. A profession must include a basic skill and some experience. Managers have many basic skills and therefore those skills could constitute the various points of first entry. But there is more to management than this. There is all that is now being taught in the business schools, consultants' training centres and in some of the best technical colleges. It should be possible now, as it has not been in the past, to formulate a second and specifically management qualification. Then finally there is the matter of practical experience. Who is to say whether a man has really practised as a manager or not? How can we achieve uniformity of standards of entry if we have to make an essentially subjective judgement? And, if we do not achieve uniformity of standards of entry, is there not some danger of bringing the profession into disrepute? I admit that there will never be perfection in judgement of practical experience, which must always have an element of the subjective. Yet, since the war, there has been growing skill in management selection and I should have thought that, given the greater accuracy of job descriptions, the limited number of companies in which a professional manager would want to serve his time, the techniques of interviewing and selection, it would be odd if a selection board for a management profession did not make a pretty good job of it. And if they inadvertently turned someone down, someone who really should have got through, there would always be another chance.

A general management qualification would be valuable in itself, but further and higher qualifications might well, for the further independence and standing they gave, be the most valuable of all and would give the chance of recognising those who had achieved real merit in management. Those whose exceptional merit was recognised by the profession would almost certainly find their way into the positions of power in their companies and companies would increasingly come to be run by professional management.

Second, there is the question of the ethical standards of the profession. A good deal of the groundwork has already been done on this. In 1951 the Institute of Industrial Administration printed a report of their Professional Standards Committee setting out a code of ethics for professional managers. This gave six main principles (the brackets contain my own interpretation):

(1) The attainment of competence as a manager to the degree requisite for the responsibility undertaken. (In other words, if you take on a job, you owe it to everyone to find out how to do it.)

(2) The maintenance of honour, integrity, and dignity of the profession. (A manager is in charge of others and he has to behave in such a way as to command respect.)

(3) The acknowledgement of management as a means to an end, namely service to all sections of the community as a social obligation. (We are there to help and not to exploit.)

(4) The recognition that loyalty to the profession is a primary duty, not to be surrendered to expediency, but maintained even at the cost of personal position and prospects. (You would sooner get the sack than carry out an order which violates the professional code.)

(5) The acceptance of the discipline of continuing personal study of the principles and theory of management and

encouragement of colleagues and subordinates to similar study. (Don't rest on your oars.)

(6) The avoidance of abuse of executive power for personal gain, advantage and prestige. (Don't throw your weight around.)

The code goes on to particularise on relations with employers and employees (you have a duty to the company, you should keep the spirit as well as the letter of the law, share your knowledge, get the facts before you act, know your employees and set them an example, remember that the company has to survive your departure); on relations with colleagues (give a helping hand to them and contribute to the general body of professional knowledge) and relations with the public (you are there to serve, you must give a hand to civic affairs and make management a social force for good in the community). This is not, perhaps, an ideal code for a full-blooded profession, but it is a basis with which few of us would disagree and which might well be the foundation for a code which could spell out responsibilities in more detail and perhaps also admit and resolve the problems a manager faces when duties to two different sets of people pull him in two different ways. Whatever we may make, buy or sell, our human relationships are fundamentally the same and we all tend to face the same sort of ethical business problems.

Thirdly, there is the problem of professional sanctions. This is a difficult and delicate matter. Yet it is part and parcel of every profession. Every year in my own profession our yearbook has a note of the number of members reprimanded and the number suspended and sometimes even expelled, with a note of the reasons. When a member is expelled it is tragic, but it is necessary, just as it is necessary to hammer a stockbroker who has defaulted in his obligations. In fact, of course, this kind of sanction operates informally at present. What else is the old boy net but some sort of protection against bringing people into partnership whose standards are not those of the others in the net? But this is hardly the fairest way of doing it. Those who are blackballed on the old boy net are tried and condemned in their absence without hope of appeal or reprieve and often on the merest hearsay evidence—or even because there is no evidence at all, just that no one in the net knows them. Explicit professional membership with standards and sanctions would make the old boy net the anachronism it is in this day and age.

There are tremendous jobs which only a professional management organisation can tackle. There are other great institutions which represent powerful interests and make, indeed, a considerable contribution to management in passing. But, in the end, they must represent the interests which support them because that is their basic business. The job of professional management, however, is to manage, and the essence of man·· agement is not the advocacy of one interest but the reconciliation of all interests. There is the overall national interest in the maximisation of economic performance, there is the interest of the shareholder in the security of his investment, in the maximisation of the net profit in the long run and the maintenance of profit and dividend in the short run, the interest of the employee in his personal income and the security of his job, the interest of the customer in value for money and the local community's interest in the company as a good neighbour. Very often these interests coincide, but too often they do not and management has to decide, without too much to guide them, who gets what.

The burdens on management are very great. One has the impression that because of the competitive structure of industry and the thick corporate veil of secrecy that this involves, every management group is struggling with bits and pieces of the same kind of problem, and that if only there were some way of our all getting our heads together, we could fairly quickly evolve some useful guidelines for a lot of awkward but soluble problems and then get on to the things which could not be solved by swapping experience but which really were on the frontiers of knowledge. Otherwise, it seems to me each tiny management team will go on floundering for ever in its own little corner of the great bog of ignorance.

It is interesting to compare the ways in which the professional civil service and industry tackle their respective problems. I know that it is commonplace in industry to mock at the civil service, and I know that it is also commonplace to say that competition is what keeps industry on its toes (though I am not sure that this is a saying of industrialists so much as of politicians and academic economists), and that this is lacking in the civil service. But I have been tremendously impressed in my year in the civil service with the smoothness of the machinery of Government (even though it was a year of great stress) and with the versatility with which the civil service can tackle the most overwhelming and well-nigh intractable problems which come whirling in from one end of the globe to the other. They seem to spend about 10% of their time in organisation and 90% of their time in tackling the real problems. By contrast, I have been struck, as I know civil servants going into industry have been, by the time taken at the top of big companies in personal and organisational problems and the tiny fraction of time left over to tackle the real problems. My feeling about this—and it can be no more than a feeling—is that the civil servant is absolutely secure in his profession and in his rank in that profession and, therefore relatively amenable to swift changes of organisational front. The manager, on the other hand, has no security of tenure from day to day (whatever the service contract may say) and there is no indication of his standing except the functional job which he happens to be doing. Every change of direction, therefore, requires a major diplomatic exercise by the whole of top management and often the full-time attention of the Chairman. I remember the Chairman of a very large company complaining that he was nothing but a glorified personnel officer and Anthony Sampson in *Anatomy of Britain* was surprised by the number of chairmen who told him that this was their biggest single job.

The civil service can bring together a corpus of knowledge and experience on almost any subject with the greatest speed, whereas an individual company will only have a fraction of that kind of experience and will spend most of its time guarding it jealously from its rivals in order to give it a bit of an edge over them. Even when a do-good national or industry organisation does bring companies together, to get information from many of them is like getting the proverbial blood out of a stone.

Competition and insecurity may keep some people on their toes and are no doubt valuable spurs but they close others up in a shell of protective security which can only slow down the aggregate of human progress. This is why we must and I am sure will have a profession of management which can help to bring together the experience of the most experienced to the benefit of all.

I leave one last thought with you. If doctors had not had a profession which put together the experience of the most experienced, a good half of us would by now be under the sod.

CHAPTER FOUR

Management Techniques and Real Life

This was an address to the Oxford University Business Summer School in July 1964, when I was still Managing Director of the British Aluminium Company. It got a pretty enthusiastic reception and some vigorous questioning afterwards—and I was asked back in 1965 and 1966—which is the real test. The talk was afterwards printed in the Journal of Management Studies.

I think that the reason why I seemed to touch a chord in the audience was because I was expressing some of the frustrations which they had felt when their idealism as professional managers had met the world as it really was.

In the case of many of the best younger managers in Britain — around the age of thirty—their enthusiasm to use all the latest management techniques has, if anything, to be restrained rather than kindled. This being so, it might be useful to look at two of major hazards in the application of scientific management to the average management situation. The greatest danger to any enthusiastic young manager, bent on applying scientific management, is that when he encounters these hazards he will become disillusioned or rebellious. The weak will be disillusioned and the strong rebellious. In neither case will he do the cause of scientific management or himself any good, not to mention the company he is paid to serve.

When I first joined the construction business, I was very keen on introducing more work study and costing to work on the site. Just think of the savings there would be if only sites were planned like factories; if they were controlled by costing based on standard man-hours for standard operations. What a competitive advantage it would give in an industry dominated by small businesses which scarcely had annual accounts let alone cost accounts. I talked to the management consultants and to computer manufacturers and they all thought that it was wide open for exploitation. But the old hands were not so sure. By all means have a go, they would say, but you could see that they were very doubtful. This, they explained, is a chancy business. One day you're in the money and the next day you're broke. The things that really make the difference, they said, are whether you have a wet summer or a dry one, whether you can get on enough short tender lists or have to tender against twenty small firms, knowing that the lowest will get the job and will then screw the price up by threatening to go broke at the critical point. The crucial decisions, they implied, were made over lunch at the Dorchester and the directors would be better advised to give their attention to whipping up a bit of profitable business instead of fussing about complicated costing and work study standards. All of this was said in good-humoured banter and no one refused to have work study engineers or cost clerks if that was what the board wanted. But they clearly did not believe that it was what really mattered.

Now, of course, one's temptation is simply to write off the old hand and press on regardless. Or, what is probably worse, to listen most attentively for the sake of good personal relations, but to take no more real notice of him than he seems to take of you. This is most emphatically wrong. The danger is that he is pointing out to you a major weakness in your theory of scientific management and you had better find out what it is before you go too far.

There are two major areas where our scientific management tends to let us down. The first is that it tends to stop short of the entrepreneurial decision, to deal with situations where all the main commercial framework is a given factor within which we have to work. The second is that it has tended to emphasise intellectual analysis rather than leadership.

When I came to the construction industry, I tended to take for granted competitive tendering, bills of quantity, negotiated claims at the end of the contract and what seemed to be the traditional pattern of the industry. My job, first as an accountant and then as a general manager, seemed to be to get the lowest costs on the job by the application of work study, method study, incentive bonuses, accurate costing, good labour relations and all the other tools of scientific management. Then we would get the work we needed by having the lowest costs and shortest completion dates. The idea of the old hands that directors should spend most of their time wining and dining customers seemed to me slightly immoral and to have very little to do with the ideal of the efficient manager.

However, theory was overtaken by the hard facts of the commercial situation. I had arrived in the industry at the moment at which building licensing was abolished and architects' offices started to pour out tenders for new work. For some reason which no one could really understand, these new contracts seemed much less profitable than the old contracts and as financial controller I had to stop thinking about costing and find out why. It was all very irritating. But it was immediately apparent that the swing in profitability was far greater than could ever be countered by the most efficient costing system. So I had to drop what seemed to me to be the real long-term jobs and concentrate on what seemed to be short-term trouble-shooting. What eventually became clear was that the industry had not allowed for the effect of the change from a regulated flow of new work under licence to the sudden flood of new work since licensing was abolished. This resulted in a bidding up of the price of labour and, even more costly and disruptive, a dramatic turnover in labour as men were attracted from job to job by the rapidly rising earnings. However, this was not at all apparent at the time. Our interim conclusion was that we should act on the basic entrepreneurial maxim that when demand appears to exceed supply, you go on marking your bids up until a balance is achieved. The market mechanism thus took over from the mechanism of Government control. Those who realised this fastest, gained far more than could have been gained by marginal improvement in site efficiency. (This leaves aside, of course, the question as to whether the decision to abolish licensing completely at that exact moment was right.)

At this point, the truth which the old hands had known instinctively became increasingly borne in on me, that attention to markets could not be neglected in favour of the introduction of management techniques; so the younger generation applied its attention to the market. Work on both went along together. But this was not the end. We then tried to apply to the market the analytical techniques more commonly used in production. This was extremely rewarding. It resulted in our setting out to sell 'design and construct' jobs instead of limiting ourselves to tender for designs by architects. The old hands had known that the nearer you were to the client the more successful the job. But they had not known why. They had simply known that when directors had known clients well, the job went well. They had associated it with Dorchester lunches. On analysis, it meant that there was sufficient mutual trust to enable the contractor to come in at the design stage, to do what all other industries did, bring the production team and design team together *before* the design had been frozen and not afterwards. The costs to be saved in economic design by using the contractor's experience at the design stage far exceeded the costs to be saved by trying to build efficiently something which should never have been built at all. The major problem of the construction industry, particularly of the large contractor, was a marketing problem, an entrepreneurial problem and not a production problem.

Once the young engineers, economists, accountants, architects and builders realised this, they brought their own peculiar skills to work and the end-product was something quite different from the Dorchester lunch. It was a package deal, a different form of contract with different relationships but specifically geared to give both the safeguards of the open tender and the lower costs arising from the award of the contract at the design stage. It did not require an old boy network to market it. It was nationally advertised and sold by direct visits from follow-up enquiries and from a 'cold' approach to likely major customers.

Shortly after I went into the aluminium business in 1960 I went to see Peter Drucker, whose books and advice I had found very helpful when I had been in the construction business. In the aluminium business it seemed I could get down to some long-term work. It was a highly capitalised industry, and much of its success appeared to have been due to the steady promotion over the years of new uses. In all his books, Peter Drucker had stressed the need for management to look beyond their noses. I looked forward to hearing what he had to say. But this was not his advice. Certainly the long-term is important, he said, but first it is necessary to survive. This seemed scarcely credible in an industry which had just reported record profits and where most outside analysts were extending the trend line to infinity. But it was not incredible to the old hands in the industry and the writing was already on the wall. It only needed a slight down-turn in the US economy and the first Selwyn Lloyd credit squeeze here to lay bare the frightening over-capacity in world ingot production and in fabricating capacity in the UK. I thought that in the construction industry, with its long tender lists and hosts of small firms, I knew all there was to know about price competition. I was wrong. Competition in an international commodity with a high degree of substitutability and fractional incremental costs was far worse. We were a low-tariff country, nil for ingot and $12\frac{1}{2}\%$ for fabricated, but even for fabricated there was a side-door in through the low-tariff Scandinavians in EFTA.

Soon after I joined the company, we started to get cut-price imports. These were based on a specialised European rolling mill producing nothing but long runs of standard products. It was backed by cut-price ingot from a European producer operating from behind a very high tariff barrier. Almost at the same time, Mr Selwyn Lloyd put the brakes on the economy and home demand dipped sharply. At this moment, too, major new rolling capacity came on stream in the UK and, as if that were not enough, aluminium ingot moved into acute surplus in the free world.

We had a look at what we could do to increase efficiency. There were cost-reduction programmes and yield-improvement programmes and overhead cuts. I asked the old hands. They looked at me sadly. We all knew that this was not the answer. The programmes went ahead, but we had to pull something else out of the bag. But the industry had practically no experience. Aluminium had been in short supply since the slump of the thirties and the answer then, the aluminium cartel, was no longer a possible solution. Nor was this the kind of thing one read about in the journals of management. We had to refer to American studies to find the model which was even remotely applicable to this kind of situation.

Fortunately, I had joined a company which had looked sufficiently far ahead to set up its own operational research unit with a small computer. We also had one or two people who had experience in other industries.

The first thing to do was to find out whether the costs of the specialised European roller were as low as his prices indicated. Our operational research unit, departing completely from the traditional overhead allocation of the accounts worked out what it would cost if we produced only long runs of standard products and put all the other costs on to the specials and small orders. The results were startling. Our specials and small orders were prohibitively expensive. Our 'long-run' costs were very low. The second decision was whether we matched the importer offer by offer and maintained prices or dropped the whole price structure on his head. The latter was, of course, much more expensive and there was a strong temptation to the former. We consulted Joel Dean's *Managerial Economics*, particularly the chapters on competition and prices and the conditions under which a trade leader in an oligopoly (four or five major producers dominating the market) determined 'whether and how to reduce the level of official prices to meet undercover concessions'. It was quite clear that the scale of competition could not be met by undercover concessions. It was also clear that undercover concessions would, if they became general, fall most heavily on the trade leader. One other point made by Joel Dean was relevant. 'The experience of many industries indicates that official prices must be cut down close to the lowest level of known shaving if price-shaving is to be dried up.' So far as we were concerned, it had to be dried up. For standard products in large quantities we cut $16\frac{1}{2}\%$. The posted ingot price, which accounted for half our costs, dropped by only 3% and this cut our conversion margin (selling price less ingot price) by about 30%. At this point imports levelled off, our market remained stable, and, as leader, we maintained our share. However, it was a tough decision.

But the imports did not drop off as we expected. The continental roller switched to low-price Communist-bloc metal and his European supplier had to match this price. We could not make up our tonnage by cut-price sales into the European producer's markets because of the very steep tariff differential against us which would have brought us to our knees in a price war. And the Communist barriers against imports are absolute. But the Communist problem was one for the whole free-world industry. Any Communist sales were a net loss to an industry already suffering from world over-capacity. It was, therefore, a problem of deciding how to conduct trade with the Communist bloc. The Europeans made demarches to the Commission at Brussels, but all to no avail. It seemed to me that there was no point in pretending that you could deal with Communist sales as if they were operating under the rules of the market economy. They had enormous capacity. They had already destroyed the market in several other commodities. In an industry where the marginal costs of extra production from under-used capacity were less than a quarter of overall average costs, they could undercut any price based on average costs and there was, therefore, no end to a downward price spiral, no point at which it would pay them to call a halt. (We could not employ the tried device of buying cut-price metal and selling it back to customers in the country of origin at the same price.) The only solution seemed to me to be that the Western European producers buy up the Communist metal and market it themselves. After considerable discussion this was agreed and after considerable negotiations behind the Iron Curtain a deal was done.

If you ever saw the Ealing Studios' Alec Guinness film, *The Man in the White Suit*, you will remember the alarmed members of the industry summoning the old tycoon to put a stop to the manufacture of the indestructible white suit. He came in an old Rolls, covered in rugs and smoking a long cigar. Old and frail, but tough and ruthless, he tottered in, found out what everyone else had overlooked, that the young scientist was under contract to the company which employed him and that they, not he, owned and controlled the invention. Cackling with laughter he tottered out to an outburst of gratitude from management and unions for having saved the industry. Although few people believe that industrial leaders are really like this caricature, this is not the role in which the young graduate scientific manager sees himself as most naturally cast. The restrictive practice of the old tycoon was undoubtedly immoral. But there are problems which have to be tackled on an industry wide basis. They should be dealt with in a framework which can take into account the public interest, but, failing an institutional framework, somebody has to take the initiative in dealing with them. Very often it is the problems outside the confines of the business which are the critical ones. Volume is the major factor in the cost of any highly-capitalised industry and a major determinant in volume is price and no one company controls prices. The major determinant in price is capacity, and no one company controls the installation of new capacity. Scientific management has to encompass the problems outside the business as well as the problems within.

How should the public interest be taken into account? The lesson which my experience has seared in on me is that the parrot-cry of 'more competition' is not the answer to the problems of industrial efficiency or of our industrial survival as a nation. It is in our national interest that we make the optimum use of our industrial investment, our commercial connections, our skill and experience and our native ability. In theory, the market economy should see that this is done and, to some extent, it does so. However, the theory of the market economy was developed when units were much smaller, when there was no widespread demand for a high rate of industrial growth, when there was no balance of payments problem and when failure of individual companies or of whole industries was accepted more philosophically than it is today. In theory, the market economy directs customers, capital and employees from the inefficient firms to the efficient, so that there is a continuance in the growth of the strong firms and a continuous decline of the weak ones. Use of the market economy assumes, however, that we can tolerate the collapse of individual firms however great our social and physical investment in them, and that we can tolerate a rate of growth associated with the slow working out of the competitive system. I do not think that we can tolerate either. Industry is becoming too complex and the investment in physical and social capital too great. It is necessary that some rational thought be added to the forces of the market.

What I have advocated myself is the formation of industry planning councils and I am glad that these have been accepted by both major political parties and that the first councils in the form of the 'little Neddies' are now in being and are starting work. I am also in favour of regional councils to deal with the very large problems of re-deployment of labour and re-training of labour if we are to attain the rate of industrial growth we need. There is little point in saying to a giant company, 'You must be more competitive', if the answer is, as press reports of July 1964 said it is, that to be competitive with American steelworks in labour utilisation they must dismiss 7,000 men. If big business is to be competitive, it can only be competitive in an institutional framework where it is possible to re-deploy and re-train 7,000 men. And the country cannot demand that business, big or small, be competitive unless it is prepared to provide this framework.

This brings me to the second hazard in the application of scientific management, which is that for every hour spent in applying your training in deciding what to do, you need to spend nine in getting it done. This is not covered by courses on communication and letter-writing or by reading books on 'how to win friends and influence people'. It is the knowledge that this is where the weight of management time goes and that ability in this field is a quite decisive factor in the failure or success of any management job, that makes the old hands sceptical of the whole business of management training. It is all right to train the army officer at Sandhurst, they say, if his men do not obey him he can shoot them for mutiny, but you cannot do that to the shop stewards. If the report about our giant company is right, I will hazard a guess that the decision that they should operate with 7,000 less men is a good deal easier to arrive at than to carry out.

If the modern world faces any challenge in the industrial field today, it is this one, how to translate what is theoretically possible with modern technology into everyday practice in commerce and industry. The countries which succeed in this will be strong and prosperous, the ones which do not, will be weak and poor. One of the major reasons for the success of the American economy is that they can take ideas generated elsewhere in the world and turn them into common industrial practice.

There is not time to spend long on this broad subject. First of all, it is necessary to know before you can do. Bone-headed leadership is no leadership at all. Lord James pointed out recently that today's leaders are no longer the Kipling heroes who went on fighting when 'the Gatling's jammed and the Colonel's dead', but quiet men who argue things out in committee-rooms. Having the right answer does not carry you all the way but it does carry you some of the way.

Secondly, it is necessary to pay great attention to detail. The reasons for most things going wrong on the shop floor, which have worked all right in the laboratory, are not usually the result of a fundamental error, but that some assumption has been made about a detail of implementation and no check has been made to see that the detail is well-founded. An associated company of the aluminium company I was in recently commissioned a £32M steel works. It was brand new and automated and utterly different from anything the company had operated in the past. They have had their teething troubles, but they were nothing to their successes. Going over their preparatory work with them, I found the one thing which stuck out was the tremendous trouble they took over detail. Delegation is all right, but effective delegation is preceded by massive labour in setting the framework and conditions for delegation. Otherwise delegation of duty is abrogation of duty.

Thirdly, it is not only necessary to communicate, it is necessary to fix the communication by some dramatisation. If you read the Old Testament, you will find that the great Jewish leaders, from Moses on, never allowed their pronouncements to go without some accompanying dramatic effect. The simpler the people, of course, the more the need for dramatic effect, but simple or sophisticated, a leader must grip people's imagination. In sophisticated argument, for instance, it is often not necessary to do more than press an argument to its conclusion. For instance, in arguing whether the builder's package deal could be launched by a long warming-up approach with games of golf, boxes at Ascot and lunches at the Dorchester, the point was settled by putting the question 'We need one half-million pound contract a week and each one will have to come from a different customer. Can this process produce contracts at this rate?' The mind boggled at a warming-up process carried on at that rate and we heard no more about it, although there had been a very strong school of thought that this was the right way.

Fourthly, it is necessary for a leader to be courageous. Those under him must know that when under attack and in a crisis he will defend them and not try to pass the buck. One of the real iniquities of the present system of progressive and effective taxation of earned income and the haphazard and ineffective taxation of wealth* is that it keeps the professional, including the professional manager, more dependent on inherited ownership than he has ever been before. The boundary between financial dependence and the bare minimum of financial independence is now almost insurmountable and there are times when the professional manager needs more courage than a more ideal balance of forces would require. But in the end, he is respected for his courage and usually none the worse off for exercising it. If the worst comes to the worst, Management Selection will usually find him another job.

Finally, it is necessary for anyone who would be a leader to respect the integrity of the individual character. People are not machines and they are not animals. They are individual souls, responsible for what they do, whether they are black or white, rich or poor, intelligent or witless. They must be treated with dignity. A leader must listen and understand and be patient and reason even when he commands. His authority must derive from his function and be accepted, not because of charismatic

* Despite the long-term capital tax, this imbalance has still (Summer 1966) not been materially altered.

qualities, but because it is seen to be necessary for the job. It is no coincidence that the countries which, in the long run, have succeeded best industrially are the great democracies and not those which ride roughshod over the rights of the individual.

CHAPTER FIVE

Managing a Business:
The Scientific Basis of Entrepreneurial Management

*This was a talk given in October 1963 at the International Manage-
ment Congress, CIOS XIII, in New York, where I was a member of the
British team of speakers. It was subsequently printed in the* Director
*in December 1963 and March 1964. The talk itself was a most un-
nerving experience. It took place in the newly opened New York Hilton
and ran concurrently with about a dozen other talks in nearby rooms.
There were about 3,000 people at the Congress, the computer which was
meant to keep everyone abreast of everything had broken down and dele-
gates wandered from one talk to another as they fancied. If you lost their
interest for half a minute they were off. On the other hand, if you had a
striking phrase as newcomers arrived in the doorway, you stood a sporting
chance of pulling them in. It was just like having a live TAM-rating.
As I gained more than I lost, the talk must be judged more of a success
than a failure. The audience varied from a director of the World Bank
to a civil engineering contractor from a Far Eastern Republic, who told
me that he agreed with my point that top management needed some kind
of information daily. His most important piece of daily information was
the rate of inflation since the previous day!*

*I include this talk because I believe that our entrepreneurial decisions
are not yet taken on a sufficiently rational and scientific basis. This is
partly because the scientific management movement has tended to concentrate on personnel management and has avoided the tough commercial
decision making process. It is also partly, I think, because commercial
decisions are so vital that businessmen have been very cautious in departing
from the well-worn path of precedent. However, the market economy is
only logically defensible on the grounds that businesses react to market
forces, to costs, competitive prices, economies of scale, growing markets,
technical innovation and the rest. If they do not react or react only to the*

last resort, then the arguments for the market economy lose a good deal of their force.

In a market economy a businessman must make sure that he preserves his position in the market-place. He has no other *raison d'être*. A state-owned enterprise has slightly more protection, but only in the short run; in the long run it, too, must maintain a competitive position. It is remarkable how insensitive the business world can be to the changing forces of the market around it. When we are looking at a situation which has gone wrong most of us come, sooner or later, to wonder why certain vital questions had not been asked. Did they never trouble to find out why the customer switched to another supplier, why they were losing staff, how their foreign competitors managed to price so much cheaper, whether Government were likely to renew their contract, what was happening to their market share? It is the first rule of top management information that it should look outwards. The director must be able to see his business in its economic setting. He must understand the place of his business in the industry and of the industry in the national economy. He must know the peculiar contribution of his own business.

If we are to look outwards intelligently, we must, of course, have a thorough knowledge of our own production process. Most of us define the scope of productivity much too narrowly. We assume a given mix of orders, a given ratio of small orders, a given time-span of order to delivery dates, a given proportion of our business bought out or subcontracted, a given ratio of manning, of yield, of idle time and given methods of production.

Our accountants then come along and enshrine these assumptions, writing them into on-costs, overhead percentages, standard costs and rigid break-even charts. The next thing that happens is that our salesmen report that some fiendish little fellow is undercutting, putting in prices which no one can match—but we comfort ourselves that no one could possibly make it at those prices. It is only when he has increased both his market participation and his profits, that we begin very tentatively to question our own assumptions.

The accountant's approach is not without its wisdom. He knows that the figures never come out quite as the engineers intended. All kinds of other costs have a way of creeping in. The only way of making sure that all costs of operation are covered is to look at historical costs and, unless given good reasons to the contrary, put them in again. But this is only an aspect of the truth. The chief executive must know what creates the costs. He must take note of the accountant's evidence, but it is only part of the total evidence. Taken by itself, it does not suggest the right answers—indeed, it may suggest quite the wrong ones. He must know, in addition, the factors which create costs, but which may not come into accounting categories. To take three examples:

(1) *Labour turnover:* In some industries, semi-skilled jobs are so routine that labour turnover makes little difference and the costs of training are small. In the construction industry, however, it is perhaps the key factor.

(2) *Cost of small orders:* Every old hand knows that, volume for volume, small orders cost more than large ones. Seldom, however, does the accountant make more than a passing concession to this truism. Costs tend to be averaged over the mix and small orders only attract additional cost where it can be attributed to them directly. The true cost can only be found by working out what it would cost to run nothing but large orders and throwing the balance of costs on to the small orders. This normally produces some startling results.

(3) *Cost of un-planned idle-time:* All the old hands know that this is high because of its disruptive effect. But few know how high it really is. As with small orders, the true cost can only be found by working out the cost of running without idle-time.

Only when the director knows all the key factors affecting his costs, can he consider alternative uses of his plant and know the degree of flexibility it gives him to match his production process with the changing demands of the market. Then what he has done for his own plants he should also attempt to do for the industry as a whole. It is not, of course, posssible to do this with precision, because precise cost information is not available for competitors' plants. But it is surprising how accurately estimates can be made. Most people know the plant in use by their competitors and the information on manning is known to too many people to be a private matter. In many industries competitors exchange the kind of information which could be found out anyhow. When he has an idea of the potential of the industry, the director will begin to see the potential strengths and weaknesses of his own company, the areas where their strength needs to be made up and the areas they can exploit more fully.

But for decisions at chief executive level, potential capacity when competitors' new plants come into commission is as important and substitutes from other industries for the product of his own industry hardly less so. A highly capitalised industry must watch for the innovation which will enable the same product to be made with cheap plant. This will enable a whole host of small competitors to enter. In the industry with low capitalisation, the smaller companies need to take care that they have the reserves or borrowing power to keep up with the mechanisation of the process and that they have the kind of staff to run more complex plant.

The most catastrophic threat, however, usually comes from outside an industry and it is quite extraordinary, looking at the past, how ill-informed those responsible for the traditional industries have been about the new forces which have threatened them. When the pioneers in road transport forecast in the 1920s the bankruptcy of the railways in twenty or thirty years, the railway industry felt completely secure in the monopoly they had enjoyed for almost a century. It is perhaps too early to be sure, but the great shipping companies may well have shown the same over-optimism in the number of passenger ships they have laid down since the war, despite the increasing reliability, comfort and safety of passenger aircraft. Many more mundane examples come to mind: the replacement of structural steel by reinforced concrete; the replacement of older materials by aluminium. No chief executive is well informed who does not at least know the basic economics of competitive industries, both old and new.

He should also know something of the economics of his customers, suppliers and sub-contractors. This will enable him to assess what can be manufactured most economically by him and what is made more economically elsewhere. Empires have toppled under the burden of the decision to make everything themselves. Others have vanished overnight when a rival has bought up a key sub-contractor. In most industries, the key market indicator is not volume, but market share. A declining volume with an increasing market share is normally a more healthy sign than an increasing volume and a declining market share. In the latter case, the business is usually in for some horrible shocks at the next decline in the trade cycle. The director should apply his skill to deciding the geographical area and the products which comprise his 'market'. He should then find some rough yardstick by which he can measure whether the share is larger or smaller than he would reasonably expect. One such rough guide is the share of capacity. If he has a 17% share of capacity, but 25% of the market, he should be doing fairly well. If he has 90% of the market, but new capacity put down by competitors has reduced his share of capacity to 50%, he will be in a very vulnerable position (even if his plant were just as modern, which it will not be). If he discovers that his share is above capacity in one product, and below it in another, he can study the possibility of bringing the weaker product into line.

It is important for the chief executive to know what is the particular brand of expertise he commands which is vital to his customers. Many companies have a level of reliability and accumulations of expertise which they squander happily on all-comers. They then find that profit margins are too tight and dissipate their one key asset in a desperate bout of overhead chopping. The chief executive must be informed on the technical needs of his customers and on the technical competitive edge which is necessary to establish his superiority in the market.

It is on the top management team that the main burden of policy planning normally falls. If they do not do it, no one else will. Other people should be capable of watching weekly and monthly variances from budget and taking action to bring affairs back under control where they appear to have slipped. Nothing is more frustrating to senior staff than to have top management turn the place upside down every month in investigation of variances—only to find, as often as not, that some dimwit has miscalculated stocks and the whole thing cancels out from one month to the next. To say that a director must be prepared to take his coat off and get stuck into a critical situation is only to say that a director must be prepared, in a crisis, to do someone else's job. And indeed he must. But if he has to go on doing this, leaving his own job undone, he should begin to wonder why he is failing to get a competent team around him. The kind of decisions which ought to be taken by the board in a business of any size will normally only have effect in one to five years' time. This is the sort of time it takes to put down major plant, to change methods of production or distribution, to develop new markets or to get the payoff from a research programme.

Information for the board should, therefore, be related to policy. It should show trends in costs, prices and volume which are significant and it should be set in the context of the published results. It should not contain the sort of detail which makes an executive director feel that he needs a couple of days' briefing if he is able to answer all the questions which outside board members may shoot, but the outside director must at least know the basis on which profit forecasts are made, the trend of business and the margin from forecast which should be allowed for factors outside the company's control.

The time-span of top management decisions may be, on average, two or three years, and the business situation demands that top management think in that kind of time-span. The capital market, however, takes account of events within a shorter time-span. A director may sometimes feel like the captain of a great ocean liner expected to make it answer to the helm like a catamaran. But he is in charge of a great deal of other people's money. There is, therefore, an area of information concerned with short-term causes of shifts in volume, costs and prices about which the executive directors must inform the board and they, in turn, the owners. The well-directed company with a sound long-range plan, with its major operations well under control and capable of dealing with cyclical variations without fuss may feel that since nothing much can be done about such short-term factors, they should not be expected to waste too much time on them. But to the extent that this ideal situation is not as common as it should be, investors' demands for short-term information coincide with operational needs and make management ask whether short-term trends have long-term implications.

The directors would, in the long term, be well advised to look at the company with an investor's eyes. It is true that it is hard, even for the investor to find a true measurement of company performance, but his yardstick of return on invested capital is difficult to better. It is certainly superior to the superficial yardsticks of growth in sales or in profits or the ratios of earnings to nominal capital. Yet it is surprising how few companies seem to feel the need to provide the same level of earnings on retained profits as they do on original capital. There is a tendency of return on capital to show a downward drift over a period of years.

The managing director should insist that all projects put up to him are so presented that they show plainly the return forecast as a percentage of the additional capital required. Unless the investment is made defensively, to protect existing investment, the earnings after depreciation must at least provide 50% to 100% more than the basic rate of interest on borrowed money, or even 1,000% more if the investment is exceptionally risky.* (If the basic rate is 6%, risk capital should aim to earn a further 3% to 6% to allow a margin for the risks which will undoubtedly eat into this target. Some risks would warrant a target of 60% over a basic 6%.)

There are various ways of making this calculation. They are, in advancing degrees of sophistication: first, a straight return on capital before depreciation; second, average return after depreciation, as a percentage of half the investment, (i.e. average book value of the investment over its life); or third, current

* Some overseas investments can come into this category.

worth of cash-flow generated (discounted cash-flow)* as a percentage of initial investment. All these methods enable comparison to be made between investments. The first will show up the proposition which will not pay off without spreading depreciation over forty years; the second is nearest to the way in which the return should affect the annual accounts; and the third is perhaps the most accurate method of comparing the projected yields of different investment proposals.

The peril of all information is that it is served up in such an absolute form. We are given the estimated yield to three places of decimals and this encourages, in all but the most hardened hearts, a feeling of assurance. When I was serving my articles with Price Waterhouse, I was firmly told by one of the senior partners always to cross out the shillings and pence in the balance sheet since they gave an entirely spurious appearance of accuracy. We even brought out figures for a prospectus for a large company to the nearest thousand pounds. All projected figures should indicate the degree of probability. For instance, a projected curve of sales might have a note that there was an 80% probability that it would be as projected, plus or minus 10%. This would, to my mind, be a fairly firm estimate!

Estimates must state very clearly the assumptions on which they are based. On what margin are forecast profits based? Is this more or less than the margin currently earned? If less, are cost reductions based on achievement or on hope; will the price hold in competitive markets or will competition react with a price-cut? How much of the added volume is based on taking a share from competition, how much on overall increase in business, how much on penetration of new markets? How firmly based are those assumptions?

It may be thought that after answering all these horrible questions, no one will dare to put any proposition to the managing director again. But my own view is that no one in the end minds the discipline of being made to do his homework and certainly no one enjoys living with the results of hare-brained

---

* Since this talk was given in 1963 discounted cash-flow has suddenly caught on and is in danger of being regarded as the only method of calculating returns on investment. But the other methods have their uses too as I have tried to show here.

schemes even if—perhaps particularly if—they were his own.

Information given to the managing director must be condensed. Condensation does not just mean the tying together of heaps of miscellaneous costs and prices for dissection into meaningless averages. It may involve giving precise information on key products or the weekly rate of yield, rejections, idletime and overtime on a particularly important piece of plant. General information might include the rate of labour turnover in key areas or the reasons given by key personnel for leaving the company. Each managing director must decide for himself, but he should try to get the kind of information which will enable him to feel the throb and pulse of the business, to know the pattern of trade and to keep his policy firmly in touch with reality.

We need to take care, too, about the mechanics of producing information. In even the best-managed financial departments there is a tendency to be so rushed by the production of returns against the deadline that there is neither the time nor the energy left to give intelligent interpretation. Ideally, therefore the interpretation of information should be separated from its production. It is also desirable that line management should, if it is to be held responsible, be allowed to contribute to the interpretation but, to keep an unbiased view, it should not have the sole responsibility.

The managing director must be particularly careful not to rely on a predigested view of every situation. He should keep open lines of informal contact with staff, labour, unions, customers, competitors (so far as the law allows), the financial and industrial press, investors and Government. He must not, of course, do this in such a way as to override delegated authority. He must, therefore, do it as far as possible to a regular pattern so that he does not appear to be going over the head of the line management on a particular issue. But if his own contact is wide and he is known not to be entirely dependent on secondhand information, there is a good deal more incentive to make the information he is given both fair and accurate.

In any case, it is highly desirable that the man at the top should see and be seen. Assessment of people is particularly difficult at second hand, and regular tours of the company's operations are a vital supplement to 'staff inventory' in picking good men for promotion.

In his personal contact the managing director should learn to listen. If he talks at all, it should be to draw a man out, not to silence him. If he is to get the truth, he must be careful not to slant his questions and he must be particularly careful not to have known hobby-horses. There is nothing more disastrous for a managing director than to be told only what he wants to hear.

CHAPTER SIX

Managing People

This talk was given in March 1966 to the Leicester Branch of the British Institute of Management. The audience seemed to be in general agreement, the main question emerging in discussion afterwards was how they could make their bosses see the light!

The management of people is so vital to a business that this book would be incomplete without a chapter on it. Yet it is such a delicate and personal matter that it is difficult to avoid pious generalities which help no one. No one can prove that one way is right and another wrong and the talk can only give one person's practical experience, for what it is worth.

When I was an audit clerk, I was always surprised not only by the difference between the morale in the different companies whose offices one visited, but in some of them I was surprised that anyone should stay one day longer. I could only assume that they stayed because they thought all companies were as bad as the one they worked in. But there are, in this country, companies in which people are proud to work, superb management teams, successful, good-humoured, secure in their relations with one another, fair to those who work for them and yet showing no signs of smugness or in-breeding. How do they do it? What are the secrets of success?

One rule I am sure is almost infallible — any company takes its tone from the top. The man who holds the top full-time position, whether chairman, deputy chairman or managing director, is the key to the management team. Union officials will tell you that they can walk round a plant and tell you, without ever seeing him, what the top man in a company is like. This is not because the board and top management say: 'I will model myself on JB.' It is because human nature finds it hard, when under pressure, not to pass on the same kind of pressure. It needs a man with nerves of iron and character of steel, when he has been bawled out, to show no signs of it to his own subordinates, to continue to treat them with sweet reasonableness. Most of us do not have nerves of iron and a character of steel. On the other hand, if you know that the one thing that makes the chairman see red is the unreasonable treatment of staff, then the reasonable treatment of staff will have a remarkably high priority. If the chairman thinks that people matter, people will matter. If the chairman thinks that the working man is 'below the salt', then, however dedicated the personnel officers and labour relations officers, there will be labour trouble in that company. You do not have to say it, you only have to think it. What's in will come out. A chairman will have the labour relations he deserves. This may sound a bit crude and perhaps it is. Labour relations in any company have a history and it takes several years for a new chief executive to change them for the better—though it normally takes only twenty-four hours to change them for the worse. A chairman of a very large company is not in day-to-day control of labour relations at a particular plant. There are such things as trouble-makers and there are no doubt those who are organised as trouble-makers by bodies other than their unions. But having said all that, I think that there is a very close correlation between the attitude of the chief executive and the tone of the company's labour relations and staff relations.

Coming down a notch from the very top—what makes the best board? Should there be outsiders as well as insiders?

Should there be one managing director with the rest answering functionally to him? Should there be a whole-time or part-time chairman? Should there be an inner cabinet? Of course, it is not possible to generalise because at this level in a company it is men who make the job and, as long as their skill and energy is there in full flood, it does not always matter too much how it is channelled. However, all else being equal, it does seem to me that there are several working rules.

I think it is generally best if the chairman is not also the chief executive. If he is, then there is no real appeal from the chief executive. Most management teams need the feeling that, in the last resort, over something which they consider vital to the well-being of the company, the view of the majority of directors can prevail over the chief executive, however exalted.

If the chairman is also the chief executive, this kind of difference cannot be settled without a constitutional crisis and possibly some resignations. It is just as well for the good functioning of the team that there should be the safety-valve of a non-executive chairman. In America the President is normally the chief executive and the board chairman is not. (When he is, he is usually specially designated chairman and chief executive.)

I think there is a good case for outside directors provided that they are people of real standing and not simply friends of important directors or those otherwise beholden to them. The test of this is whether they can resign without difficulty. If they cannot because their part-time job is an important proportion of their income and they would find it hard to get another on the same terms, then the chances are that they are there to throw their vote behind someone and that they are not there for their independent advice. This criterion goes for some full-time directors too. But the outside director who is on boards of other companies of similar standing can prevent a management team from becoming too in-bred. He can help the general process of cross-fertilisation of ideas and can often help with some particular expertise of his own. Few companies of any size have completely inside boards. I understand that one of the few large American companies with an inside board, Standard Oil, have now appointed some outside directors.

Having said all that, I am afraid that a great many companies do still tend to appoint the wrong type of person as an outsider. The outsider really needs to be more of a professional than the insider and most people seem to agree that too many are still too amateur. It needs the professional to stand up to the expertise of the insiders. He needs to be able to see the wood and not the trees. He must be able to pick the figures to pieces, to get behind the guff of the reports, to shake complacency if it needs shaking, to reassure whose who are shaken by the holocaust of events—if they need reassurance. Too often, however, the outsider is not a professional at anything, not even at being an out-sider, but is the amiable, hail-fellow well-met, who is appointed because all the board happen to know him.

How should a managing director fit in with the rest of the board? In a very small company there is only room for one dynamic individual, though genuine partnerships of individuals can be found in small companies as well as big. But in a company of any size—with a labour force in thousands—I am sure that management must be a team-affair and that the managing director must be to the executive directors as a first among equals and not as a boss to subordinates. Certainly there must be a chief executive, someone must chair the management committee. But no one should feel that they cannot take a contrary view to the committee's chairman or argue with him. Most sensible managing directors should feel rather alarmed at the thought that their word alone ended the argument. A lot of nonsense is talked about management by committee. Of course, there should be a line of executive responsibility. But right at the top, where the critical decisions are made on which the whole future of the company will depend, there must be some drawing together of the best brains of the business and some resulting consensus which everyone is prepared to support.

Even in executive direction of the business, I believe it is a mistake to be too tidy-minded. There should certainly be a laying out of the direct lines of responsibility. No one should shirk the task of putting down on paper who answers to whom and for what. But the fact is that our skills do not blend with each other in practice in quite the watertight way the neat little boxes in the organisation chart would suggest. Human relationships are much more subtle and if we are really to present them graphically there should be more variety with thick red lines as well as thin red lines—not to mention those familiar dotted lines which show a general interest. The civil service have a good phrase to indicate a line responsibility where others, nevertheless, have an interest. They ask: 'Who is in the lead?' This implies primarily responsibility but not exclusive responsibility. It may well be that a rigid line structure with everyone sticking strictly to their little box of responsibility is an easier system to operate. It is certainly better to lay down responsibility than to leave it to sort itself out, allowing the self-assertive and domineering to push his way through the pack. That way lies chaos. But once a board have recognised that there is a problem which requires conscious thought, they are half-way to solving it.

The first rule of team-play is that there must be mutual trust, the second that there must be mutual respect. The third is that players should have certain primary positions, the fourth that they should—on the analogy of tennis or football—be flexible in adapting those primary positions to the exigencies of the moment.

Trust in a management team cannot be laid on to order, but it is the responsibility of the chief executive to see that it is fostered at every turn. If he is ruthless in this, he can be amiability itself in all else. No one should feel his position threatened by being left out of key discussions. There should be no inner cabinet. No one should gain an advantage by putting his side of a case in private. No chief executive should 'divide and rule'. There should be open and frank discussion.

Mutual respect is harder in some ways than mutual trust. To be trusted we only have to be honest for long enough. To be respected means that our contribution to the team must have a certain quality. This is why selection of a top management team is so important. It only needs one poor player to wreck a team. On the other hand, many an indifferent player has been transformed by playing with a good team. Probably the most important guide in picking a team is to get the balance right. There has to be a mixture of old and young, high flier and steady runner, thruster and parrier. There has to be a decent representation of all sides of the business, properly matched, and of the different kinds of skills, technical production, commercial, financial which go into a business. People are a bit more inclined to respect the skills to which they lay no claim themselves. But include two or three salesmen all bent on showing who is smartest and you are heading for trouble!

Perhaps the highest skill of all is to maintain the discipline of separate responsibilities and yet be certain that there is enough flexibility to ensure that the team can help each other. There is nothing worse than dealing with a business where there are rigid demarcation rules. Mr Jones deals with this and no one else can. Mr Smith deals with that and does not want his colleagues to invade his private preserve. Our merchant banks have many faults, but you always have the feeling that if you deal with one partner you are dealing with all. No doubt it is against all the text-book rules to have ten managing directors, but at least it makes the customers feel that whoever they see is the chap that matters. But once let someone in the team take advantage of the openness of the arrangement to build his own empire and the whole scheme falls to the ground. You do not mind your partner dealing with your prime responsibilities in your absence so long as he hands them back intact when you show up again. But, if the game suddenly becomes like musical chairs where a visit to America leaves you out of the circle just a fraction too long, then everyone will start to stick very closely indeed to his chair.

The civil service is extremely flexible. In the service almost everything for which you are responsible is dealt with in your absence. The Queen's Government must be carried on and will not wait for your return—often it will not wait twenty-four hours. If you come back later and think the wrong decision was made, that is just too bad! But, in my experience, you do not usually need to complain because the team is a good one and not only knows its business, but knows the mind of its absent colleague, respects his views and tries to take into account the view he would have given if he had been there. This is the sign of a true partnership.

Business life is, by its nature, insecure. We live in a competitive world and it is likely to get more competitive, not less. Business has to adapt, and sometimes rapidly, to changes in the market. The skills which were needed ten years ago are not relevant today and today's may seem irrelevant in ten years' time. Businesses cannot carry passengers and yet people need to be secure in their work. This goes not only for the man on the shop floor, but for the man in the management team. How can we keep the security that is needed for good morale and mutual trust, the security that is needed if men are not to take defensive action to preserve their position and yet keep the flexibility that is needed for a changing business world?

I am sure that the answer is not to guarantee employment for life. It is certainly not to keep a man on until he is fifty because you do not have the courage to tell him that he should find another job and then find you have to fire him in the end because you must have an overhead cut or go under. It would have been far better for his prospects of another job if you had let him go when he was five years younger. Even if you are financially able to keep him on to retirement, is it really showing respect to a man's personality and spirit to keep him for twenty years of his life in an irrelevant job? Maybe it is your own fault, maybe you over-promoted him and he has not been able to stand the pace. Is it not better for him that before he gets all kinds of chips on his shoulder, you should give him a clean break and a chance to start on the right level somewhere else?

All this may sound hard-hearted—just a rationalisation of the brute facts of taking a man's job away. Indeed it can be done in a hard-hearted way and on hard-hearted conditions. But it need not be done that way. Most enlightened companies today give pretty generous severance conditions and plenty of chance to look round. In conditions of full employment, it is rare for anyone under fifty—certainly for anyone under forty-five—to be left for long out of a job if he really wants to find one. However, there should be certain known safeguards before anyone is asked to find another job. This decision should never be made by the man's immediate boss alone. Any 'life or death' decision should be taken two up the line and with the agreement of the personnel officer responsible. Possibly it should be taken by more people, but, in my judgement, three should be the minimum. It is also wise to make sure that most other people in the management team will regard the decision as right. If it is on business grounds, then this should follow logically from a known business situation and not appear to be an arbitrary and isolated move. If it is on personal grounds, then most other people in the team should feel, after the move has been taken, that it was a case of the wrong man in the wrong job. If it has not become generally apparent, then it is best to wait a little longer. If in doubt on these critical personal matters, it is better never to rush. If it is the wrong man in the job, this will eventually be plain to everyone. If it is just a bad patch, then everything has been gained by waiting. It may seem to be costing thousands of pounds while you wait, but the loss of morale is a move which makes the rest of the team feel that they are threatened will cost far more in the long run.

Those who are within six or seven years of retiring are in a different category. Here it is clear that they will not do another job at the same level and that their career will be brought to a premature end. They may well have served the company faithfully for forty years. Is it right to turn them out into the cold before their time? Many companies have their own way of dealing with this. Some have special jobs which are created with light duties and high-sounding titles. Some wealthier companies retire on full pension at sixty regardless. Some have arrangements between the two, involving part-time duties and a lower salary. What I am sure is wrong is to keep a man on in a job when he is quite clearly beyond it. I remember once arguing that a man of, I think, fifty-nine should be retired on full pension. Tremendous technical changes were taking place in his department and he was quite clearly out of his depth. His boss argued strongly that he had served the company well and though he was not in his prime, it would be morally wrong to retire him. In the end I had a generous proposition worked out and put it to the man to see what he thought himself. He was overwhelmed with relief. He told me that his only son had been killed in an accident a few years before. Since then he had been quite unable to concentrate. His memory had started to go and all the changes in the department had been too much for him. The more he worried the worse he got. Later I met his wife at a company function and it was clear that an enormous burden had been lifted from both of them. Not every case is like this, but my guess is that, of those in the wrong job at the end of their careers, more men than would openly admit it would be glad of an early release.

The really difficult time to change is between forty-eight and fifty-eight. It is too early for premature retirement and often too late to get a comparable job. This is all the more reason for making changes when they can be made. But if they have not been made then, if the company can afford it, it should, in my view, try to make the best use it can of the managers it has got. If a man has been with a company for any length of time, there must be many a useful job he could do. Even if he is not in line for management, there are probably a dozen assignments which he could do with profit to the company. There must be few companies which have no creative outlet for men who have worked their way up the ladder. These assignments need careful thought, for they are not usually thrown up by the day-to-day pressures of business and if they are not tailored both to the man and to the needs of the company, they can simply degenerate into unproductive overhead. But if a man has given so many years' service, the company owes it to him to take a good deal of trouble to work out a job which he can do and which will be of use. When politicians are promoted to the House of Lords they only get £4 14s 6d a day during sessions. We usually have to pay more, so putting it at its very lowest, we should see that we get value for the money.

Last, but not least, there is the job of putting the management team together. How many people should a growing company take in from outside? Should a company aim to grow all its own timber? What are the rules for a successful promotion policy? What span of control should be allowed to one man? What should be the depth of management hierarchy? These are large questions, but perhaps I can leave a few notions with you.

Taking people into management team from outside can be a tricky business. There is a natural predisposition against it. A newcomer is always, to some extent, an unknown quantity. All the existing relationships are slightly altered and some are altered a good deal. People take a long time to give their confidence to newcomers. Some come and go again without ever receiving it. I was once told of a plant in a large group which was never very successful. The latest in a line of plant managers told some of the men what they should and should not be doing.

One of them gave him a long hard look and said in a fatherly way, 'Look, chum, we've been here twenty-five years, we've seen chaps in your job come and chaps in your job go and some of you say this and some say that and we reckon that long after you've gone, we'll all still be here and still doing it our way'. And so they were.

That is one end of the scale. The other end of the scale is the company which boasts that it never takes in outsiders. In some ways this is fine. But what it means is that no one in that company has any first-hand experience outside its bounds. However big a company, its bounds are small. A company employing 2,500 employs only 0.01% of the working population. It is not a wide enough band from which to draw all the experience you need in a competitive world. A friend of mine interviewed the other day a key salesman in a company which has been very successful in its particular line of business, but which grew all its own timber and was proud of it. That this young man was at that moment a crack performer in the business in which he had been brought up, there was no doubt. But he had been conditioned to run one kind of race and one alone. On a different kind of course, with different conditions, he would have been completely outclassed. Not only was he no good at all outside his own company, but one day the market in which that company itself operates will change. The army of specially bred, specially conditioned executives will, like the German Army in 1914 after the Schlieffen Plan had failed, and the French Army in 1940, after the Maginot Line had been outflanked, suddenly find itself fighting a war quite different from the one laid out to the last detail in the minutely exact blueprints.

My own experience, therefore, for what it is worth, is that some leavening from outside, some cross-fertilisation, is not only desirable but also most necessary. Furthermore, I do not think that it is quite the hazard it once was. Since the management selection consultants came on the scene, it is much easier than it used to be to find a fair selection for any job and the chances that you will land with someone completely hopeless are much lower. Mind you, you still have to watch it. I was once helping a colleague to select the final short-list. We were told that the candidate we were to see next was 'though fifty-seven, still capable of playing a lively round of golf'. The fact that my colleague was fifty-seven and still capable of climbing· the Matterhorn put us slightly off our stride, but when he arrived, he looked sixty-five, if a day, would not admit that he was as deaf as a post and treated us to a long and rambling discourse on how he had been 'bypassed again and again', given an honorific title and a splendid office and no work and now wanted to get back into the saddle once more. Well, I'm afraid he was bypassed once more and it was quite a while before we used that lot of consultants again.

Having said that, I am bound also to say that this was an exception and that over the last ten years I have found management consultants and management selection consultants extremely useful in finding first-class men to some very special specifications. If a man is in a fairly good job he will hesitate quite a long time before he answers a public advertisement. He regards it as a major move. He does not regard a letter to a consultant as more than a minor move. In the latter case no one knows except the consultant that he has made the move and indeed no one need ever know whether he approached the consultant or the consultant approached him. In the one case he has to make a personal commitment before he is in the market, in the other he can be in the market without any commitment at all. The consultant is, therefore, able to make a far wider trawl than is ever possible to the individual company. This is not a commercial and I have no interest to declare.

Even if we do take some leavening from outside, most of our management team will have made their way up the company ladder from inside. I am strongly in favour of making this as short a ladder as possible. There should certainly never be more than seven steps to the very top. If this is enough for an army it should be enough for a limited company. This means that the span of control has to be wide. The wider it is, the less a boss can breathe down the neck of any subordinate and this is excellent.

I am not, however, in favour, as a general principle, of

chucking people in at the deep end. Everyone deserves a good boss, even if not everyone needs one. We all want someone to go to with the really tough problem, someone to agree on our objectives and what is a reasonable performance, someone to defend us higher up the line. But then most of us want the freedom to get on with the job without too much fussing. If our boss has eight to nine other chaps to look after, he is unlikely to have time to fuss over us, but if he has only one or two then life can be one long fuss. A broad span means that management objectives have to be spelt out and this is good. (I would like to make a bow in the direction of 'management by objectives'. I am sure that this is the only way to manage.) But above all, a wide span and a shallow hierarchy helps to sort the men from the boys. Annual performance reports written up once a year by a man's boss and the personnel manager are useful in a limited way, but are bound to be somewhat subjective. What is needed is the objective standard of a man's actual performance on the job. Agreed that some have tougher jobs than others. Some ride on their predecessor's performance. Some may be lucky and some unlucky. But I think that there is a lot in Napoleon's saying that he only promoted those who seemed to be lucky. We all have our opportunities. The good manager is the one who is ready to take his chance when it comes, who can see it before anyone else and who knows what to do when he gets it. Those are the men to promote. Those are the men who give the team its *esprit de corps*, and if anyone knows where to find some, perhaps he will let me know!

CHAPTER SEVEN

Business Professions Old and New

This talk was given in the Autumn of 1965 to a combined meeting of the Chartered Accountants, Certified Accountants and Cost and Works Accountants in Belfast. Because I was speaking to fellow members of my own profession and because of my concern for the future of our profession, I was a good deal more forceful and critical than an outsider might have been. Although it was a speech by an accountant to accountants, the effect of the speech was something of a shock. It was not at all what had been expected and the audience was divided between those who wanted to see change, who spoke up and those who would have been responsible for making the changes, who seemed to think it best to hold their fire! Even those who wanted change found it hard to see the market for a new type of business advice from the clients on their books. Yet, with assistance from the Northern Ireland Government, other business consultants were already taking on a rapidly increasing business in Northern Ireland.

I have included this talk because one of the themes of this book is the need for more professionalism in industry and it is only right, therefore, to look at the professions, especially some of those closely connected with industry and to look at the way they work. There is no doubt that professions can suffer from some hardening of the arteries as they get older. On the other hand, there are always new professions thrusting in where the older ones have failed to take their opportunities and forcing the older professions to adapt or to bow out. Professions are, for the most part, democratic institutions and their members are quite capable of seeing that they keep up with the times, so I don't in the least despair of them, least of all do I despair of my own profession.

Nineteen years ago, when I took articles, the accountant dominated the industrial scene. Businessmen took the advice of their auditors on most of their major commercial decisions and newly-qualified accountants were snapped up right and left by industry to go into key jobs. The other professions were hardly in the race. They might be consulted on their specialities, but hardly on anything more and seldom on broad business strategy. Today accountants no longer have a monopoly. There are now a number of other professions which give advice on general business strategy. There are the business economists, the management consultants, the merchant bankers and most recently, but perhaps ultimately the most potent of all, the operational researchers. All of these make it their business to look at overall strategy and none is too strictly confined to their expertise. Their expertise is a means to an end and they are interested in the end rather than the means. Twenty years ago none of these professions was at all strong. Today they are all fairly well established not, it is true, with a Royal Charter, but perhaps most important, they appear well established in the minds of ambitious young men who are looking for a profession which will take them to the top in the minds of company directors who want their businesses to have the kind of advice which will ensure success.

On the other hand, the accountants, wherever they have had to choose between their function as an auditor and their function as an industrial adviser, between their secure legal status and their more uncertain industrial status, seem to me always to have come down on the side of their securely established legal function as auditor.*

Perhaps I am being unfair in this. It is hard to prove. But there is at least some evidence this way. First, there is the proportion of practising accountants—and this, in fact, means auditors—on the Council of the Institute. This does not reflect the proportion of accountants in industry. I think that well over half are in industry (only 11,000 out of the 39,000 members are

---

* Of course, the function has to be fulfilled and it is true to say that the new complexities of tax and other fiscal legislations have left practising accountants, particularly the small ones, with little time to spare. The President of the Institute is currently making representations to Government on this subject. There is a widening range of Government Departments now concerned with fiscal matters such as Investment Incentives, (BOT) and SET (Pensions and Labour). Increasing demands are being made for 'accountants certificates'.

in practice in the UK and I doubt if many of the 5,000 overseas are in practice). As far as is known an even higher proportion of young accountants are going into industry, so that the future pattern of the profession will be heavily industrial in membership, but despite those high proportions in industry only a small proportion (7 out of 50) of the Council are industrial accountants (though the proportion of Council seats given to accountants in industry may, in the future, rise from 14% to 25%). Second, it is extremely interesting to look at the way in which the profession tackles the technical point of depreciation. We all know that with the fall in the value of money, the amount set aside in depreciation is inadequate to replace the asset at the end of its life. For this reason, companies' pricing policies aim to recover more than the depreciation charged in the accounts and the cash-flow is always kept higher than the total depreciation by plough-back of net profits. Even the Inland Revenue now give allowances 30% higher than the cost of the asset.* And if they are persuaded to give away the Treasury's money you can take it that the argument has substance! Despite all this, we accountants still continue to charge historical depreciation.

Now this has reason. It is not obscurantism. It is because, as auditors, we are recording angels. We have to account to the shareholder for what the directors have done with the money and once you start messing about with the value of assets in the balance sheet, putting in replacement cost rather than historic cost, you start to obscure the historic accountability and make the auditor's job of putting a true and fair view to the shareholders more difficult. However the static or auditing function has, here as elsewhere, triumphed over the dynamic function of commercial and industrial strategy.

In many ways this choice is understandable. The auditing function is absolutely secure. Every company must have its

* This was written before the introduction of Investment Grants. There are sound reasons for relating depreciation to cost in financial accounts — not necessarily in cost accounts however — and it is universal in the USA. However, accountants concur in the revaluation of fixed assets and in providing additional depreciation above or below the line so long as it is clearly described. There are also arguments against recognising 'inflation depreciation' as an element of cost.

auditor by law and the auditor must not be subject to dismissal by the directors because he has to report to the shareholders on the directors' use of shareholders' money. There are, therefore, the strongest safeguards on the auditor's tenure of office. But when he advises on business strategy he advises the directors and he has to compete with all the other professions who are in this field. Given a secure and necessarily uncompetitive market and an insecure and highly competitive market it would be less than human not to give more weight to the former. Nevertheless, one would have thought that those accountants not in professional practice, but in industry itself, would have made their weight felt much more.

The greatest difference I can see between the accountants on the one hand and the business economists, the merchant bankers and the operational researchers on the other, is that the expertise of the accountants has been based on the company and the expertise of the latter is based more widely and cannot, indeed, be applied to the company without putting it into its context in the whole economy, the whole capital market or the whole industry in which it competes. The accountant is accustomed to work with the figures which arise within the company rather than figures outside the company, to which he has no right of access. The whole expertise of the business economist, of the merchant banker's investment analyst and of the operational researcher is to construct estimates and models from such figures as are available and his skill depends on his judgement in picking the significant figures and in testing his models to make sure that they are sufficiently accurate for the purposes for which they are used. In considering business strategy it is quite essential to take into account the situation in the market among customers, competitors and suppliers and it is more useful to concentrate on the key factors than on the mass of information available from within the company. The accountant's basic expertise has been inward-looking and the other is outward-looking.

In a company which I once had to advise, there was a plant which made the final product which badly needed modernisation and a number of plants making the products earlier in the stage. The two groups of plants were not quite balanced and because the company needed modernisation in the final product they were losing market share and had a surplus at the earlier stage. The internal approach tended to be restrictive. The company simply didn't have the money to modernise and, therefore, there was nothing it could do but await better times. However, the merchant banker said that to secure its future it *must* modernise. Furthermore, since it had excess capacity in the earlier stages it had under-utilised assets. If they could not be used for this purpose there might well be another purpose for them. If there were, then they had an inherent value which did not depend on profitability of the company and so he could raise money on them. They did have another purpose no one had thought of (because the company hadn't looked outside its own business) and it was clear that money could be raised on them for twice their book value so that, though they were not short of ready cash and credit, they could safely embark on their modernisation programme. But they could never have embarked on this programme without looking outwards.

The business economists are still fairly rare but their numbers seem to be growing fast. The kind of thing they will do for a business is to have a look at its market and say whether it seems, on the available information, to be losing or gaining share. They will try to pick the markets which are significant to the company from which its real bread and butter comes, without which its business would not exist. They will then estimate the output of its rivals over a period of time, compare it with its own business over the period and highlight the points at which they were making inroads on it or it on them. They will then try to relate the swings on the graph to the known business decisions — the bringing in of this new product line, the dropping of that old product line, the strike in plant A, the falling off of quality in plant B, the setting up of an import agent by foreign rivals, the decline in your customer's share of *his* market, the stockpiling stockdrawing cycle. No longer is the board content with hearing the sales director say, 'Well, volume's keeping up', because they know that there's a good deal more to it than that. What is happening to imports? What capacity is being put down in Germany and will the growth in the German market be able to absorb it or will they have to sell some over here to get their plant beyond break-even? But it is when we come to the field of capital expenditure that the economists are really breaking new ground. Today capital investment is not just a question of money and faith, it is a highly sophisticated exercise. It has to take into account the likely growth of the whole country, the related growth of the industry, the capital investment intentions of competitors, technical innovation and obsolescence, the likely trend of prices and wage and raw material costs and the alternative investments which might be made with the money.

Even taxation is no longer the accountants' preserve. It is significant, I think, not only that one NEDC investigation found that a great many businessmen did not take investment allowances into account in making their investment decisions,* but that the main exponent of 'discounted cash-flow', which does take tax into account was not an accountant but a business economist.

In the old days when a company wanted an internal reorganisation it called in one of the doyens of the accounting profession.† Today it is as likely to call in the doyens of management consulting. It is, of course, quite true that accountants do not purport to cover the whole range of the large management

---

* Not all accountants agree with the NEDC report that businessmen did not take investment allowances into account. The large ones especially say that they have never met a businessman who wasn't fully alive to the importance of investment allowances and their effect on capital expenditure and claim, probably with some justice, that by their ingenuity they have widened the application of such allowances, for example, in the growth of plant leasing. They feel that the NEDC pamphlet on DCF overlooked the need of the director of a public company to know the effect of capital expenditure on his Profit and Loss Account and of all businessmen to forecast their cash flow.

† It is difficult to speak of the 'profession' collectively since it comprises a host of sole practitioners, many small firms and then the medium and large size firms. Many of the small practitioners can give only a restricted service to industry, mainly on tax and auditing, but the very large firms do give a wide service far beyond these subjects. Consultancy has grown steadily and many companies who wish to retain their existing small auditors, employ the larger firms as consultant and this includes advice on mergers and organisation as well as finance and capital expenditure.

consultant, who will have specialists on industrial engineering, marketing, labour relations, training and organisation as well as on management accounting. But even on his own field of management accounting, the accountant is sometimes passed over in favour of the management consultant. This may not be justified, because some accounting firms have, in fact, developed excellent management accounting services. But not every accountant has learnt how to give the most useful kind of advice. The fault, where there is one, seems to be that the traditional accountant starts off with the auditor's training and instinct that he is a recording angel and must make sure that all transactions and especially all expenditure is properly accounted for and that the final record given to the board is comprehensive. They may agree, reluctantly, that a summary is needed though ideally, as one once told me, the management should not grudge an afternoon a month trying to get to grips with the figures. The summary is, however, often accompanied by massive documentation and one company director reported that the whole thing had to be brought into the board room in a wheelbarrow!

The management consultant (who is as likely incidentally to be an accountant as an engineer) does not start by collating and summarising the information available. He usually starts from the other end. He tries to find out what the management need to know. He realises that there is nothing more aggravating than to be faced with a mass of information which does not suggest any particular action. It may signal disaster ahead but will give no guide as to how to avoid it. The management consultant tries to find out what yardsticks management is accustomed to use. What are the key ratios in the business? Is it stock turnover, rejection rate, labour turnover, hours of overtime, process yield, sales volume per customer visited, order mix, hours of unplanned breakdown? On the shop-floor are the old hands who will tell him that if they keep their eye on this or that key ratio all will be well. The good consultant does not, of course, leave it at that. He will want to test the validity of the theory, to find other key ratios, perhaps to make some rough model of the process. But, in the end, where the weekly or monthly control document comes to management, it should be in language which they understand and where there has to be a translation from their familiar ratios into money terms. It will start from the familiar ratio and lead to the unfamiliar money implication so that they can measure the unfamiliar financial implications of the familiar workaday decisions.

This is perhaps the point at which to mention another skill with which the economist and industrial consultant are increasingly familiar, but which some of us still handle reluctantly and uneasily, that is the skill of graphical presentation—what one consultant likes to call 'figureless accounting'. It is a fact that most engineers and chemists, not to mention salesmen, are far more at home on graph paper than they are in columns of figures. If an engineer wants to illustrate a point he instinctively reaches for his block of graph paper and draws it. So, if we want to illustrate a point for him, we should draw it too. But how many of us, in fact, know the knack of graphical presentation? Should you show actual orders received, three month moving average or annual moving average? When should you use geometric graphs and when arithmetic? When should you show growth rates from a base date of say 1958 = 100 and when should you show actual levels? (If graphs of British growth were based on actual levels instead of putting every country, however backward, on a level with us in 1953 or 1958 or whatever, we would get a far truer picture—a picture of countries catching up from much lower levels instead of countries appearing to soar ahead.) The great beauty of graphical figureless accounting is that—thoughtfully and wisely done—the picture which emerges, the upward or downward trend, one line overtaking another or two lines diverging, the shape of the cost/volume curve—all these present both the facts and the implications at once. They also give a much better idea of relative quantities and, therefore, of relative importance than figures do. It is interesting that a journal like *The Economist* gives almost all its figures in graphical form. It also had, in one Christmas number, an unforgettable article on how to mislead through graphs. To minimise a decline you stretched the whole graph sideways, to exaggerate an increase squeezed it together and cut off the bottom. But nervous practitioners afraid, above all, of not giving a true or fair—if dull and unintelligible—view, should not retreat from the art but should master it.

Finally, let me come to that subject of all speeches today, computers. We all know that this is revolutionary, but it behoves us as accountants to understand why. What is so novel about the computer is not its use as a business machine to do better and faster what the punched card did before it. What is really new is the computer as an aid to the skill of business decision-making, known as operational research, which is also new. Like so many good things this was a British invention developed by the Americans. From a tool of military logistics they turned it into a tool of business decision-making and it is now back with us in that guise.

Operational research is the application of mathematics to the known factors in business problems in order to find the best solutions in varying circumstances. From the pattern of the operation, whatever it is, it tries to create a model which will show how output will vary with different kinds of input. This model is usually expressed as a mathematical formula. This is seen at its simplest in queueing theory. You have a given number of access points to a bridge or a quayside which can take a given volume of traffic. The operational researchers will study the pattern of traffic presenting itself, the hold-up points, the time spent at each, the interaction of the traffic streams in various access routes on each other. It will then build a formula or model which, in any given situation, will tell you how to direct the traffic for the fastest throughput in the prevailing circumstances.

A more complex application is the routing of a mix of orders coming into a plant. The OR model of the plant will tell you which orders to aggregate into long runs and which to put through first, which to make on which machine in order to get either the fastest delivery time or the optimum profit or a pre-determined mixture of both. But, whereas the simple model can be done by mathematical formula, the more complex ones are best done by computer, which is ideally suited to this kind of exercise. In what it does mechanically, the computer is no more than a beefed-up punch-card machine, but its memory is 100 to 1000 times greater in capacity and it can put everything through at the speed of light, so that it can give a whole range of answers which were never open to punch cards. In particular, it can match the input with its whole memory in say half an hour, so that you can re-schedule your complete order book every day to get the optimum output in time and profit. In the British Aluminium Company we did this twice a week in our tube and extrusion plant. We also used it to judge the weekly load we should put on our Highland smelters, which relied on hydro-power from local reservoirs. The reservoirs could not maintain full load throughout the year and we had the option of drawing down the reservoirs, cutting load or buying out power. The computer memory contained all the rainfall statistics for the catchment area since the last century and fed in rainfall expectations for each month, the actual rainfall from our gauges, present furnace load, relative costs and so on to give the optimum path. (However, you always have to watch your basic data. A neighbouring landowner once told me that he thought our chaps had been poaching his deer so, in retaliation, he had filled our mountain rainwater gauges to the brim. He said 'I bet that gave your computer hiccoughs.')

All this may sound a bit technical, but occasionally a technical innovation does have revolutionary implications and this innovation is one of them. We are so bombarded with publicity about revolutionary machines in general and computers in particular that we may discount it. But, professionally, we would discount this at our peril. We still don't know quite how to use or control these gadgets in making industrial decisions. It is a very tough job to put them in because it requires far more analysis and questioning of existing methods than anyone has normally had time to do. But just for that reason those who master this machine and methods of operational research are going to be so far ahead of those who have not yet tried that it will be almost impossible to catch up with them again.

You may think that all this is outside the accountants' field.

Let's stick to our cost accounts, our ledger columns, our tax computations, our estate duty and insolvency. But the accountants' training is incomparable and far too good to waste. We are trained in the strict discipline of analysis. We learn how to pull things apart and find out what's at the bottom of them. We are trained to be exact, not to give generalised by-and-large answers to hard questions. We are trained to be honest and to give a true and fair view. I have had an academic training and an accountant's training and there is no doubt that it was the accountant's training which stretched my mind and made the little grey cells really work for the first time. We do not indulge the academic pastime of seeing every possible and impossible side of a question and refusing to come down on any. We are practical men and practical men have to make up their minds to a view and act on it. The consultant is important but he doesn't live with the decision afterwards as the financial director does. The merchant banker, in the nature of things, sees the problem from the City and the operational researcher is not so broad in his training. None of these alone can displace us and my advice to you is that more of us should add some of this new expertise to our own (as many accountants have already done). Those who do this have an unbeatable combination of advice to offer to their industrial clients.

Addendum

I have included this talk to show how some business professions work in practice, but also to show that professionalism is competitive and, therefore, adaptable to changing conditions. The talk was, in some respects, one side of the argument and it would not be fair to the accountancy profession not to mention some of the changes it is making to adapt its services to the needs of the time. It has been announced that discussions are proceeding between the Institute, the Scottish and Irish Institutes, the Association of Certified Accountants, Cost and Works Accountants and the Institute of Municipal Treasurers and Accountants with a view to amalgamation and a complete reorganisation of the accountancy profession. This is a far-reaching proposal promulgated by the Institute of Chartered Accountants and is now under consideration by Government Departments. This would result in wider training facilities in industry as well as in the profession and emphasises the Institute's determination to keep the profession in the forefront in the modernisation of business.

The rules of the Institute of Chartered Accountants have recently been altered to add another 10 members from industry, making a total of 15 out of 60. The Institute now has a wide range of lectures and courses on Electronic Data Processing and has recently established a Certificate and Diploma in Management Consultancy open to all qualified Chartered Accountants. Some accountants have established computer bureaux and a number of the larger firms of accountants have joined the Management Consultants Association. Professional management accountancy firms offer a wide range of services beyond the staple diet of budgeting control, stock systems and management information and include on their staffs engineers, economists and other specialists. (In one major accountancy firm's Management Consultancy Division less than half the specialists are Chartered Accountants.)

I can, perhaps, best conclude with comments on the profession from two members of the Council who read the text of the talk.

'Accountants, particularly those trained in practitioners' offices, have been slow to see and grasp the opportunities for widening the scope of their services, but immense and not unsuccessful efforts have been made in recent years by all the professional accountancy bodies to change their members' outlook.'

'Naturally I am prejudiced in favour of the professional accountant and as a partner in one of the largest firms I admit that our experience is not necessarily typical of the profession as a whole. But I do a great deal of work for the Institute and have a fair knowledge of what is going on. I know we have too many small units and not enough firms big enough to give specialist services, but overall the larger firms give a wide constructive service to industry which is limited only by our success in recruiting suitable personnel in competition with industry and Government bodies. The whole profession is on the march with the possibility of achieving the greatest change since the inception of the Institute in 1880.'

CHAPTER EIGHT

The Company's Place in Society

*This talk was given to the British Institute of Management, South
Western Branch in Bristol in the Autumn of 1965. The idea of a
Chartered Company is not new and I owe a good deal to George Goyder
who in his book* The Responsible Company *has outlined a much
more detailed scheme than I put here. I have concentrated on the need
rather than on the exact blueprint, though I am inclined to think that
what is needed is a Charter to be awarded to companies who meet certain
specified standards, which also gives to the directors the right to call
themselves Chartered Directors. There would also have to be Trustees of
the Charter to keep the company's performance under review and possibly
a special position in law for the Chartered Company.*

*If we are to have more professional management, more scientific
management, more rational commercial decisions, good and enlightened
leadership and intake of the best of the country's talent into industry,
with proper promotion and training in industry, and if we want respon-
siveness to national needs as well as to the immediate needs of the
company, then we should at least question whether the nineteenth-century
version of the limited liability company is the very best institutional
framework. Those who feel that there should be some diffusion of
economic power in a free society are therefore set looking for a means to
make thousands of centres of economic power responsible to society for
the objectives and standards on which society rightly sets store. The fact
is that many companies do in practice behave in the most responsible way.
This talk suggests that the standards of these companies be set as the
ideal and that those companies which can be shown to recognise them
should themselves be recognised by society. This may not be a very
revolutionary suggestion, but it seems to me to be very practical and, in
the society in which we live, and which is very alive to public recognition,
likely to be effective.*

I have gone in some detail into the arguments against the development

*of full-blooded American anti-trust legislation in Britain and this may
give an appearance of being altogether against competition as an aid to
economic efficiency. In fact my belief is that competition is a spur to
efficiency in the long run and if tariff barriers come down we shall have
more of it in future and not less. But what worries me is the tendency of
many people who have never themselves been responsible for commercial
decisions to rely so heavily on the theory of competition for improved
productivity. Unless we realise the limitations of the theory and practice
of competition, we may not see the need for alternative methods, so I
have taken some trouble to show the limitations of the competitive theory
as I have found them.*

*The talk had a good response and apparently caused a good deal of
discussion afterwards.*

Most of us today take the limited liability company as one of
the facts of life, part of the scenery which has been there for as
long as anyone can remember. But it is not much more than a
hundred years since the liability of companies was limited to
the called-up capital and scarcely fifty since shareholdings in
the larger companies became widespread. Yet today, the great
corporations are amongst the most powerful institutions in the
land. Will they continue to hold their place? Will they grow
more powerful still or will they, like so many other great institutions in the past, decline in power until they become no more
important than a livery company?

When you look at a flourishing enterprise, it is always useful
to try to cut through the foliage to find the real roots of power
and growth. Companies do not flourish by some sort of natural
law. There are quite identifiable forces at work and if these
ceased to operate, companies would decline. First, the company
is based on statute law. The common law rule was that a man
who traded alone or in partnership was liable for his own debts
and the debts incurred jointly by him and his partners. That
was the 'natural law'. The company had to be given the special
protection of statute law before it could exist in its present
form. From being the sum of its partners the company took on
a separate legal being, a life of its own, even against the partners. This law was passed mainly for convenience and to

enable enterprises to become as large as was economically justified without being limited by the sum total of the partner's fortunes. This need for scale still holds. It is unlikely that enterprises will become smaller.

Secondly, the company can be directed by professional managers and does not have to be directed by the owners. Only if the owners have a major stake in it do they take any active part in its direction and even then they may still leave it to the professional managers.

Thirdly, the economy is so complex that it is very hard for anyone who is not actively involved in the business to question the decisions made by the directors so that, within the limits of their economic resources, they have very considerable freedom of action. Only in the rarest cases have the shareholders or the state been prepared to take on the responsibility which the directors exercise.

Fourthly, the other powerful group involved in industry, the unions, have not been prepared to take initiatives. Their strategy has been, except in matters which directly concern them such as wages and conditions of work, to leave the initiative with the directors.

Fifthly, the tax system and the fall in the value of money have encouraged the ploughing back of profits and the resources of companies in real terms have increased over the years.

Sixthly, competitive forces have operated unevenly in many industries since the 1930s and demand has been persistently ahead of new investment, giving high utilisation and a lesser incentive to compete on price. We have had the application of Keynsian economics to expand overall demand without any similar intervention to make sure that physical capacity expands in time to meet the demand.

Finally, the discretion in the hands of directors has enabled them to outbid Government and other institutions for staff and services.*

Despite these and other powerful forces, all reinforcing each

* Despite their ability to outbid Government and the professions by quite a high margin, industry still, as I have tried to show in chapter one, finds it hard to get the quality of management it needs.

other, company directors are not really established in society in the way in which the Member of Parliament, the doctor, the lawyer, the schoolmaster, the mayor and corporation, the sailor and soldier are established. In part this is due to the attitude of the educated Englishman to industry. We have been a great imperial power and the offices of state and administration mean more to us than seats on the boards of commercial concerns. In part it is because companies have not been going long enough. In part it is the secrecy and apparent self-interest arising from competition between companies. People on the whole prefer co-operation to competition when it comes to things that really matter and competition which affects the livelihood of families does matter very much. But, perhaps most important of all, there is no generally accepted philosophy of the company, nothing but plain economic convenience. For a powerful institution to be accepted by society, there must be some philosophy which gives a meaning to its existence which the ordinary man can both understand and welcome.

The nearest we come to a philosophy is the idea of co-partnership. This meets most people's philosophic demands and yet it has not met with general acceptance. The reason for this is, I think, that it makes the basic mistake of trying to reconcile divergent interests not directly by negotiation but indirectly by trying to subsume one in the other. While the worker's wages from employment are so much greater than his dividend as a shareholder, his major interest is simply too great to be subsumed. It will always pay him to have his employee's hat on and never his shareholder's. Again, the co-partnership idea presupposes a continuing relationship. But, though there is a core of steady employees in most companies, there is altogether too much mobility between companies to make co-partnership a convenient scheme to operate. Mobility is part of a dynamic society. The main thing against tied pension schemes and stock options is that they pin down in one company scarce skills which might be better used elsewhere. Either co-partnership has this element of constraint which is economically undesirable —and perhaps socially undesirable too—or the shares are freely saleable, in which case it is not co-partnership but another form of cash bonus. Nor is it a good thing for a man to have both his job and his savings at risk in the same enterprise. One of the few contributions I remember being made by the union representatives on a works pension trust fund of which I was chairman was a plea that none of the trust funds should be invested in the company's shares. They had enough at risk in the company without putting in their savings too. In a dynamic economy the best managed companies will be subject to the hazards of changes in supply and demand and it is a good investment rule to spread your risks and not to concentrate them.

In Germany each company has to have a given number of trade union representatives on the board. This gives a formal voice in the management to the unions. But, in practice, the board on which they sit is, I believe, a rather formal affair and the real decisions are taken by the full-time management of the company sitting on a separate executive board. In practice, therefore, the unions have little voice and I understand that the jobs are held as sinecures by elderly unionists who are generally regarded by the rank and file as having gone over to the other side.

My own view is that the respective interests of employees and the company are sufficiently different to require their negotiations with each other for all practical purposes as different interests. But they have enough in common and are sufficiently interdependent to give them an interest in agreement—unlike the trustees of charities who often have only fractional economic reasons for agreement and the highest and most enduring moral reasons for continuing their differences to the last ditch! But this does not mean that their interests are the same and, in this sense, there are and always will be two sides of industry.

Even if all were well between employer and employee the company needs to find its place in society as a whole. Indeed, were the interests of the employer and employee to be miraculously combined, as the syndicatalists would have them combined, they would prove an even more powerful force in society and there would be the more reason for society to bring the company to terms.

There are, today, two rather different philosophies of the

corporation, but neither is applied wholeheartedly in Britain. There is the Russian philosophy where the need to have a separate interest is denied. The interests of the state and the interests of the corporation are declared to be one. However, it seems that the Russians are finding that this declaration is not enough. If you put men in charge of economic resources and give them control over funds—and they must have some control over funds—you create a separate economic centre of power, and this will be so whether the state or private citizens have the right to the residual profits and the power to appoint and dismiss the management. The Russians' new look at the profit motive shows that they are now having to negotiate at arm's length with the industrial powers they themselves have created.

The other philosophy is American and is embodied in their Anti-Trust Laws, the Clayton Act, the Sherman Act, the Webb-Pomerene Act and the Robinson-Patman Act. The philosophy behind these acts is that a company has the right to make what profits it can so long as it provides goods or services at prices which are governed by competition with other similar companies in the open market. This is easy to say, but fairly hard to spell out in practice as the vast case-law of anti-trust proves. It is also difficult to enforce without the ultimate sanction of imprisoning otherwise worthy citizens whose only sin is that they talked to each other about their firms' commercial intentions. However, no jury will convict an otherwise worthy citizen except on the most unimpeachable evidence and firm evidence that two citizens of a free country talked together about one thing rather than another is not too easy to come by. But the real complication of anti-trust is that, except in the very long run, the issue in competition is decided not by current average costs, but the ultimate strength of financial resources. Consequently the Sherman Acts having laid down at the turn of the century the original premise that companies must compete on price, the Robinson-Patman Act had to be introduced to protect the less financially well breeched from those whose reserves of cash enabled them to exercise economic dominance by means of price wars.

If company A, with a broad product range wants to take

company B's market for its major product, it can drop its price for that product to an uneconomic level and temporarily cross subsidise from other products. Company B, with only one major product, is helpless as its business is taken away and eventually it has to sell up for a fraction of its worth. The most likely purchaser for the assets may well be our old friend company A which thus recoups its little outlay and, provided it buys the assets and not the shares, may well escape the anti-trust section of the Sherman and Clayton Acts. Robinson-Patman, therefore, comes along and says that price cuts must be based on costs and not on discrimination in the market. This means that your price movements are subject to question by anti-trust and you must not only record them, which is not too hard, but also be prepared to justify them. However, this leads to one other complication. What happens if your salesman in Minneapolis reports that he is meeting Japanese competition below your list price. If you can only justify a price cut on costs and have to prove that it is not discriminatory, do you have to see your Minneapolis business go to the Japanese or lower the price from coast to coast? Well, the case-law says that you can lower your price to a group of customers without altering the price list for all customers, if the alteration is made to meet competition. But even this produces complications because a shrewd and not too scrupulous buyer will often report that company X has cut its price, so company Y's harrassed salesman reduces his price to meet, as he imagines, his competition. Then company X is shown company Y's quotation and he, in turn, meets a competitive price! From that point on no one really knows who is making competition and who is meeting it!

I leave aside for the moment the laws which aim to prevent a company's having too large a share of the market. That American industry flourishes is, I am quite sure, in spite of the Anti-Trust Acts and because of its enormous technical and managerial strength. In fact, of course, it does not take the law to its logical conclusion as the dominance of the giants of American industry like General Motors, AT & T, IBM, General Electric, Westinghouse and Du Pont indicates. But I would beg those who think that the way to lay hands on our enormous industrial opportunities is the simple pressure of economic competition to study the case-law of American anti-trust when they will realise that this is, in fact, an immensely tangled and difficult subject; it is only a means to an end and it is not at all clear or proven that it is the best or most direct means to that end.

There are two other points to be made about self-regulation through competition.

First price competition, where financial resources are equal, is based (in all but the very long run) on marginal costs and not on average costs. In the old days the sunk costs in equipment and buildings were a relatively small proportion of total cost, so that the difference between average and marginal cost was not great. Labour and material utilisation was the biggest part of cost. However, as capital cost per employee goes up, the proportion of sunk costs becomes greater and the marginal costs of producing an extra ton or a thousand foot run or a million gallons become relatively unimportant. Price cuts have to be enormous if they are to get down to marginal costs and so the penalties of price war are enormous too. The real economics of the operation are decided in the design and in the research and development of the product, not in day-to-day operation. So price competition, because it can be suicidal even for an efficient firm, becomes an increasingly irrelevant weapon with which to enforce economic efficiency. I have no doubt that this is why real price competition—though it does happen—is increasingly rare. It may be the ultimate weapon, but like other ultimate weapons, it tends not to be used.

Secondly, with the gradual lowering of tariffs, the formation of EFTA, the increasing ease with which highly capitalised industries can take tariffs in their stride and with our heavy dependence on international trade, we simply cannot afford to lose out to international competition. Not only does this mean that we have to have companies which can match the resources of our international competitors in scale of operation and of research. It also means that we cannot stand by while these companies are overwhelmed by international competition. Our national survival depends on their survival.

We may hope that in the jargon, 'The cold wind of competition will wake them up!' But the time lag today between the research and investment on the one hand and the successful marketing of the final product on the other, is so long that if a company has not kept up with research, development and investment, the show-down in the market may be final and the cold wind of competition will simply blow over the corpse of a once-great company. This is not fanciful speculation, it is already happening.

Having spent a great deal of time in knocking down other philosophies, it remains for me to put forward the one I find most practical in the world of today. I suggest that what we need to do is to look directly at the ideal end product and then decide what it is we want to do to attain it. Fortunately the ideal end products are not far to seek. Our trouble in Britain is not that we have not got very fine companies, it is that the average is well below the best. So let us look at our better companies and see what they do and then see how we can encourage others to do the same.

What is it that the country as a whole wants from the good company? First it wants a company which will train the skilled workers and managers for the future, although it knows that it will not get the benefit of all these workers and managers itself, because once they train, they may go elsewhere. It is a company therefore which benefits from and is not burdened by an industrial training levy. It not only trains in mechanical skills but in all the human skill and thoughtfulness which goes into successful industrial relations. Its management training scheme does not consist of taking on a given quantity of graduates and sending them round to 'sit next to Nellie' and learn what they can. It gives them real jobs as soon as possible, it has a proper ladder of promotion, takes care to see that they learn and are not frustrated and that they are taught the skills which will be needed in ten years' time and not the skills which went out of date ten years ago. The ideal company releases key men to go on management courses and does not whip them off at the last moment to deal with a panic situation.

Second, the country wants a company which has a proper

machinery for joint consultation on all matters which affect those who work for it, so that those who take the ultimate decisions know what really goes on on the shop floor and so that those who represent the employees know that management will take them into discussions on all major changes in their plants which will affect the pattern of life of the employees and will not tell them at the last moment when nothing can be done about it.

Third, it wants a company which, within the limits of what is economically possible and even slightly beyond those limits in times of real need, will do its best for the country's balance of trade. It wants a company which invests for a world market and not just a home market demand, which gives as much weight to export sales as to home sales, which if it cannot for the moment meet its needs from home suppliers will do its best to see that its future needs can be supplied from the home market. It wants a company which does not try to keep its capacity fully loaded by restricting new capacity.

Fourth, it wants a company where, at the very top level, the management is professional and seen to be professional by everyone in the company, where no one feels that he will be cheated out of a board seat because he is not related to the right people, does not know the right people or talks with the wrong sort of accent.

Fifth, it wants a company which is a good neighbour, whose smoke and effluent is not just this side of the law, which plays a constructive and helpful part in civic affairs, where the directors are not remote, but are approachable and know the local personalities.

Sixth, and especially important, it wants a company which knows its business, knows its markets, knows what its customer wants today and will want tomorrow, knows the latest techniques and technology in its industry throughout the world and has the courage to try not only those techniques which have been proved, but also to prove some which have not; a company which, because it is efficient, can pay for its wage increases out of increases in productivity and still have enough over to give the customer better than average value and the shareholder better than average returns; a company which, because it is efficient, is not worried about the marginal extra costs of being a good citizen.

Seventh, it wants a company which because it has the freedom to pay high salaries and therefore can attract more than its fair share of the country's talent, will not begrudge some of the time of its top executives in the service of Government, but will willingly give part of their time and energy to the national good.

You may think of other things the country might want from the responsible company, though these are, I think, some of the most important. But even if there are more, I am not being idealistic and fanciful. Such companies exist in some numbers. I know this, because part of my job is to obtain from industry help for the Government which only industry can give. Not only do these companies give most generously, but they seem to be none the worse for it. In fact, the better the company's economic performance, the greater seems to be the effort it can put into strictly non-economic efforts. The more dismal the company's economic performance, the more dismal the help it gives to anyone else. Economic performance and public spirit appear to be indivisible.

It seems to me that if the community decides that there are certain standards it wants companies to keep and certain things which it wants them to do beyond the letter of the law, then it should say so; that having said so it should accord some explicit recognition to these companies, so that everyone knows who they are and so that those who work in them and those who direct them can be proud not just of their economic performance, but also of their public service. There has been some good-natured mockery of the Queen's award for exports, but I guarantee that no company which receives the award will fail to display it and no man who works in that company will fail to tell his wife about it.* I also hazard a guess that if a company

---

* This has been borne out since the first awards were announced in 1966. I visited a small company in Hudderfield recently and both the management and the main union representative said that they were sure most people in the town knew about the award and that it was making a real difference to morale and recruitment.

obtains public recognition for its economic performance and public spirit, it will obtain more than its fair share of the national talent and that in that event neither the customers nor the shareholders will suffer for the cost of its public-spiritedness. I also wonder, and this is no more than personal speculation and to be taken no more seriously, whether if we had a takeover bid for a company with a fine record (including a good economic record) and which had been publicly recognised by an award or a charter (or in whatever way recognition were to be given) and a bid was made for its shares by a *mixum gatherum* financial empire, the Government of the day would really be allowed to stand by and see it disappear into the maw. If people are proud of an institution, it does not lose its independence too readily. Look at the loyalty of citizens to their city or borough in the reorganisation of local government!

If there were full public recognition of these pace-setters and of those who directed, managed and worked in them, would there not be the strongest urge on others to try to obtain the same recognition? Man lives by bread but not by bread alone. We need decent incomes and most of us want more than we have, but the extra effort is not pulled out by money alone. We also need a sense of purpose and recognition in our daily work, and if we are given money instead we often spend it simply to buy the recognition which a more sensible society would have given for nothing.

But, in any case, we owe it to the self respect of British industry, which has taken some hard knocks, to recognise those who have earned that recognition by both their social and their economic performance.

CHAPTER NINE

Macro-economics — the National Plan

In the next part of the book we move from action by industry to action by Government and since I was a civil servant the tone of the talks naturally had to be different

The first talk was given to the London and South Eastern Branch of the CBI in November 1965, a month after the publication of the National Plan and the second talk was given to the Glasgow Branch of the CBI in January 1966, shortly after the White Papers on Investment Grants and on the Industrial Reorganisation Corporation. Both talks were well received and well reported. Both the Investment Grants and the Industrial Reorganisation Corporation are supplementary to the action list in the Plan and that is why I have added extracts from a speech in which I explained their purpose.

At the date of going to press it is quite clear that the most publicised part of the National Economic Plan, the 25% growth between 1964 and 1970 cannot survive the Government measures of July 1966. I was at first inclined to think that there was therefore not much purpose in retaining in this book a speech on the Plan, but having read it through again, it seemed to me that the points which I had made about economic growth needed to be made all over again and that to check the Plan against what had actually happened gave — as a check on a good Plan should — the clearest possible indication of what had gone wrong and what therefore had to be done to put it right. A Plan is partly a prediction, partly a series of decisions aimed to achieve the prediction and partly a benchmark against which both the predictions and the decisions can be measured to see whether they need to be changed. It is now clear that the original prediction has to be changed, but what is vital is not whether growth in that particular quinquennium was 5% or 10% out, but whether the equivalent annual rate of growth can be sustained, whether 4% is achievable whether — as I believe — it is too low or whether it has finally been proved that Britain

inevitably grinds to a halt as soon as the growth rate goes up beyond 3%.
It is extremely difficult to be steady in a crisis, not to react emotionally,
ready to analyse the figures and to decide coolly and objectively just what
did go wrong. But this is the only sensible thing to do.

In this speech I pointed to the various improvements which were
necessary to put our balance of payments on the sound footing needed to
establish the economic growth which has so far eluded us. I made the
point that the Plan was not just a series of statistics but that it must also
be a plan for action. I argued that the key improvement now necessary
was not on the trading account, but in the non-trading items in the
balance of payments, defence and capital outflow. I said that there
was every hope that the main trading item — exports — would run at
the 5½% annual increase shown in the Plan. Finally I said that though
incomes had risen well above the norm, prices had held stable and that
it was vital that prices should hold until the rate of increase in many
incomes eased.

What then went wrong, what lessons does it hold for the future and
what prospects are there of our attaining that elusive rate of 4% sus-
tained growth — or even of improving it?

First of all exports, up to the last month before the crisis which was
distorted by the shipping strike, had gone even better than predicted.
1965 was 6% up on 1964 and the first five months of 1966 were 9%
up on the first five months of 1965. The decisive indicator of our
national competitiveness, our ability to hold our own in export markets,
was much better than before.

Incomes policy had not gone as hoped. The rate of increase in money
wages did not ease off and gradually prices, which were fairly steady
for a long period, began to show the strain. Whether or not there is a
strong correlation between the rate of wage increase and export com-
petitiveness, the international financial community certainly believe that
there is and although the wages increases did not reflect in our exports,
they did reflect in financial confidence in Sterling. The Government in their
endeavours to bring incomes back into line suffered a long shipping strike
rather than concede what they regarded as an inflationary wage increase and
they pressed ahead with the Prices and Incomes Bill at the cost of a major
cabinet resignation. The 1966 budget following the 1965 budget
brought the total amount taken out of the economy in two years to the
highest figure since the forties, so that, before the crisis, the Government

seemed to be taking such steps as they reasonably should to make sure that the rate of increase in money wages did in fact ease.

The Plan was farthest off course on the capital account. Although the reduction in portfolio holding was yielding over £80M a year, inward investment had slowed down and, more serious, outward investment kept up at the high 1964 rate of £400M right through 1965 and into the first quarter of 1966. The net outflow in 1965 was about £175M against the target net inflow by 1970 of £75M, a total of £250M off course and showing no sign of improvement. It was clear that the measures in the Plan had been well short of what was needed and in the April budget the Chancellor introduced a system of voluntary guidelines for investment in four major countries in the sterling area.

The Plan had aimed to reduce the rate of overseas defence spending and aid roughly by £50 to £100M and the aim of the Defence Review had been to consolidate total Defence spending at £2000M. The cuts were to come later in the Plan period and meantime the rate of Government spending overseas continued at about £550M. However the Chancellor, after the election, started negotiations with Germany to eliminate the £90M currency cost of the Rhine Army and the Secretary of State for Defence announced the reduction of the forces in Malaysia to the pre-confrontation level, though without specifying the exact monetary cut.

Despite the good export figures, the deflationary budget, the Prices and Incomes Bill, the tough line on the shipping strike, the extra balance of payments measures both on capital account and defence, July nevertheless saw a very heavy withdrawal of 'hot' sterling and a consequent covering of currency commitments which together mounted into such a run that the Government had to take further crisis measures at the cost of the 25% growth target in the National Plan.

What are the lessons and how can we recover the growth rate?

The real lesson of the crisis of July 1966 is that if our current allocation of national resources does not give us enough liquidity without uncertain foreign help and prevents us from expanding at more than 3% a year without running short of liquid funds, then we had better make up our minds once and for all that we must change our current allocation of resources until we have the liquidity we need. With a gross outflow of almost one billion pounds a year (Private overseas investment £400M and Government spending £550M) it is within our power to change our *liquid resources considerably inside two years. If we have put the strength of the currency ahead of the growth of our industrial resources, then we are at least entitled to put the growth of our own industrial resources ahead of some of the demands made on them by third parties.*

If we do this, I can see no reason why we should not set our planned rate of growth and why, having set it we cannot resume our overseas responsibilities on a far more stable and reliable basis. We can plan to be a strong industrial power or a weak imperial power. It is now clear that we cannot plan to be both.

The trouble with a word like 'Plan' is that it can mean so many different things. Some people associate it with the controls and allocations which have gone with wartime plans. Some people associate it, though this is not what the word means, with predictions as to the exact course of future events. Some seem to think that since life is uncertain there is no purpose in having plans. It is much better to think up something to meet the crisis when it arrives. 'Sufficient unto the day is the evil thereof.' However, I imagine that most people in responsible positions are, in fact, well accustomed now to planning for several years ahead. We all know that making a plan does not make our wishes come true, but it is much more likely that the majority will come true if we set out exactly what it is we want and have some sensible and considered plan of action to achieve it. This is what the Government have tried to do in the National Plan.

What I imagine most people want is not a discourse on the nature of planning, but to be able to judge whether the figuring is firmly based, whether the programme of action is likely to achieve the aim of the Plan and finally what magic there is in it which is going to give Britain the economic growth which seems to have eluded her since the war. Perhaps this last point is the most important of all. When all your business experience for twenty years has been to one recurring pattern, it is extremely hard to believe that that pattern is not set by some pre-ordained law of nature and is just as changeable as everything else in this changeable world.

First of all the figuring. I remember some worthy Member of Parliament once expressing doubts about business forecasts because you could not predict the Beatles or the fashions of the mods and rockers. And, of course, there is a fringe of the economy which cannot be predicted, where what is bought depends almost entirely on personal whim. But I do not think that this worries EMI.

They do not know what will be on the gramophone records, but they do know they will be cutting records. Nor does it worry the tailors of Carnaby Street. They do not know what shapes next year's cloth will be cut into, but they do know they will be cutting cloth. The National Plan, I am glad to say, will not be shaken if skirts come down to the ankles or the Rolling Stones cut their hair. There is a great deal of flexibility in the consumer end of the economy and it can take short-term shifts of demand in its stride. It is when we get back to the heavier end of the economy with a high capital to output ratio that the predictions matter more. What will be the demand for steel, for oil, for coal, for chemicals, for engineering, for roads? All these require long-term investment. We have to begin deciding now what plan we will need for the 1970s. It takes longer and longer to design and commission complex industrial plant and as the costs rise of single projects, the financial penalties and rewards become much greater.

A large part of total national investment, about 45%, is, in any case, in the public sector and this is fairly predictable. The programme for roads, houses and power stations, for military expenditure and for education is laid down in advance and it is, therefore, of considerable benefit to the industries who sell immediately or ultimately to Government to have the Government's expenditure plans set out in some detail. This is, perhaps, the most firmly based part of the figuring, and one of the Plan's greatest uses to businessmen. But it is on the private sector forecasts that most people want reassurance. So many business-men are known not to make long-term predictions. Even the predictions of the best businessmen are known to go astray. However, most of the big businesses do now do five-year forecasts and have accumulated quite a lot of skill and experience in doing so. These businesses account for a very consider-able proportion of industrial production especially in the less

flexible heavy industry and, in any case, when a trade association is putting in the industry figures it will know which
forecasts come from experienced companies and which do not.
I very much doubt, therefore, if the predictions are really based
to any great extent on the figures of inexperienced companies.
Although it is true that even the best individual companies'
forecasts are often out, this may be because of gain or loss of
market share, and the figures for the whole industry are much
more likely to be accurate. (Indeed, it is hard for any board of
directors to accept figures for loss of market share.) Again most
people look at figures annually and the figures over a five-year
period even out year to year fluctuations and are much more
likely to be right than the figures in any particular year. The
Plan does not purport to show the annual figures. Finally, any
attempt to co-ordinate forecasts of inter-dependent industries
by giving an overall target of 25% and by relating industries to
each other, is in itself—provided the target is realistic—a built-
in stabiliser in attaining the overall target. It is interesting to
note, as I pointed out in the *CBI Journal* earlier in the year, that
the last Neddy Plan was, in fact, remarkably accurate both by
industry and in overall growth. The only trouble was that it was
only too accurate. It predicted the annual increase in exports
at only 3% but said that if the plan growth target was to be
reached they would have to go up by about 5%. However
exports went up by only 3% as industry had predicted. This
time I am glad to say that industry has predicted that exports
will go up by 5½% and the rate taken in the Plan is slightly
lower, 5¼%. It is early days yet, but so far exports are doing
remarkably well, being 6½% up in value over last year on the
nine months to date.*

I must, of course, add that the figures in the Plan have been
checked by Government economists and put through the computer programme known as SAM (Social Accounting Matrix)
at Cambridge. Anything which looked odd has been discussed

---

* At the date of writing, Spring 1966, exports are still doing well, the largest and
most unexpected adverse swings on the balance of payments seem to be coming
not from our trading performance, but from capital account and defence. It is
only fair to say of course that there is still a large deficit on *visible* trade, imports
still being on the high side.

with the industry in a so-called dialogue and the figures have been altered where necessary. Finally, we amended some figures to take into account the Chancellor's July (1965) measures, although these did not worry us as much as they seemed to worry some people and, so far, our own more optimistic estimate seems to be right. So much for the figuring.

A Plan is not just a series of statistics, it must also be a plan for action. Even though the figuring shows that we have the resources to put the balance of payments right and get a 25% growth in real output, it is not enough to leave it at that. We must make quite sure that this time it really happens.

The Plan, therefore, contains a check-list of the actions to which the various parties are committed. Of these the most critical section is on the balance of payments. This is the section on which, since the war, we have always come unstuck, so we have to be sure that the action this time is enough to see us through.

It is important to realise what is and what is not important in the balance of payments. It is more within our control than sometimes appears. Over the last five years 1960 through 1964 —a period of two balance of payments' crises, we have had an annual surplus on visible and invisible trade of over £200M. We export four times as much of our GDP as America and half as much again as the Common Market. Our main trouble is not, therefore, that we are deficient on trade. We can and do pay our way in the world as a trading nation. Our main trouble is that this surplus is not enough—just as America's surplus is not enough—to carry out the other commitments in which we are involved. These are mainly three, first of all our heavy commitment on defence of about £250M; then our overseas investment, which has amounted to £4,000M since the war and for the last five years run at over £300M a year.* Third, there is aid which is running at about £200M. These items accounted for more than the total of last year's deficit.

The point to bear in mind when people criticise Britain's

---

* The net overseas investment (deducting investment in the UK) is lower, but the total of British investment overseas is now running at a much higher figure, nearer £400M than £300M.

industrial performance is that none of our trade rivals except America bear these burdens. What we have invested abroad, Germany, Italy, Japan and others have invested in their own home industry. We guard the trade routes for the increasing exports of our rivals while, because of this burden we cannot afford the industrial investment to maintain our own share in world trade. We invest heavily in the development of other countries and see our own investment-starved industries run out of capacity every time demand is allowed to go ahead. Our basic problem is not wage inflation and industrial stoppages, nor is it activity rates. Almost every other major industrial country has a higher rate of wage inflation and America, which has, up to now, controlled its wage inflation with 5% unemployment, has two or three times our wage level. Most other industrial countries have a worse record of time lost in strikes. The main exceptions are Germany and Sweden, which at any rate in the 1960s, have paid for it with a higher rate of wage inflation. People complain that we run the economy with an unemployment rate which is far too low at 1·5%. But the German rate is 0·7% and the Swedish rate is also lower. We have one of the highest activity rates in the world. We have more people at work and they work longer hours than in most other industrial countries. We have tremendous industrial opportunities. We could do far better than we do. Once we can see our way out of our balance of payments difficulties and have confidence in the future, I am sure that productivity will rise and we will have a higher annual growth than 4%.

What the Plan proposes however is to rely on no more than industry's own forecast of exports to improve the balance of payments, but to put in hand a number of measures which will, at worst, make sure that this is attained and, at best, see it comfortably exceeded. However, Government has taken direct action on the major causes of the balance of payment's deficit, especially on capital investment abroad. The aim is to improve the net balance of private capital account by £150M a year which, given the average annual figure of over £300M private overseas investment for the last five years, is a very substantial contribution. To achieve this improvement it is also intended to take steps to restore the inwards flow of permanent long-term new industrial investment and this will give a positive balance on the capital account. The restriction on overseas investment is not, of course, welcome to those companies operating overseas, but we cannot continue to invest abroad by increasing our short-term borrowing. The measures on capital outflow and the inflow to the reserves of a quarter of the proceeds of all portfolio sales are working according to plan.* The defence review is now in progress and the aim is to save £50M to £100M.† The annual outflow is now running at about £250M, so that taking into account the difficulties of running down existing commitments, this is an appreciable saving.

We will still have to make our contribution to maintaining the peace of the world. But it cannot continue to fall on us and on America alone. Finally, there is the level of aid which is being held to a small rise over the levels in the current financial year which was about £190M. This has meant a very strict limitation of aid to existing commitments and without going back on these no lower level was possible even if it were desirable. We have, of course, a very strong moral commitment to aid. For the future it is the intention to see that the aid we do give has the minimum impact on the balance of payments.

These three improvements together with the forecast balance of trade will be enough to fulfil the Plan if exports rise as industry has predicted. But a number of steps are, nevertheless, being taken which will, I am sure, improve on this forecast. These are all down-to-earth measures. They do not rely on exhortations to patriotism — though we should not minimise the efforts which have been made and are being made from pure

---

* Although this source alone now seems to be providing half the improvement necessary, overseas direct investment had not been reduced by the time of the 1966 budget and the Chancellor therefore took further measures to restrain overseas investment by introducing a voluntary guidelines policy for the four major developed countries in the Sterling Area.

† The defence review announced cuts east of Suez, including the Aden base. However the Plan was produced prior to the Rhodesian crisis, which must have had a noticeable effect on the balance of payments. On the other hand, at the time of writing it looks as if the expensive confrontation between Malaysia and Indonesia is about to come to an end.

patriotism. One of the most important steps is attention to the detailed improvements needed to speed up the movement of exports. Ability to quote quick and reliable delivery is one of the major factors in making a sale—more important often than price. Stock locked up in transit is a dead loss to the economy. If we could reduce the pipeline by one week, we could lay hands on £100M foreign exchange to add to the reserves. For this reason we have set up the little Neddy for the Movement of Exports and it has special mention in the check-list. It will do something no one has done before, co-ordinate the efforts of all those through whose hands exports pass from supplier to final customer. Without this co-ordination the technical innovations which should revolutionise the transit of goods would never get off the ground.

Another hard-tack project mentioned in the Plan is the Export Corporation at present under examination by a sub-committee of BNEC under Sir Charles Denman. I understand that this sub-committee will be reporting fairly soon and I do not want to anticipate its findings.* I can, however, outline the object of the exercise and I think I can also say that although there are still problems to be overcome, personally I believe that they will be overcome. The object is to set up a corporation in the UK which will buy as a principal and not as an agent (so relieving the smaller businessman of any further responsibility) on short or long-term contract and, if possible, at base-load prices, goods for which its market research has found an outlet in world markets. It is thought that this is the best way to get the smaller manufacturer into the export market on a long-term basis. He would not have to go abroad himself. All his marketing and selling would be done for him. He would simply have to sign a contract in the UK with a UK corporation. Most export merchants buy and sell as agents and would not have the financial resources to enter the market as principals on the scale required. This institution would, therefore, fill a

* The particular scheme examined by this sub-committee encountered difficulties in applying the idea to this range of products in one of the 2 markets which they were examining. On the other hand several EDCs have shown an interest and my view is their Export Corporations will probably be set up for particular industries.

big gap because most of our export trade is done, as everyone knows, by the major companies. I have been told by our Embassy in Washington that too often the small British manufacturer will sell a line of goods in a trade fair in, say, Minneapolis or St Louis. The goods are right and the price is right and American buyers have told the Embassy, when they have followed up trade fairs, that they would like to buy more but that the supplier never turned up again. Apparently the supplier did not have the experience to follow up. I shall be surprised if this project does not make a major contribution to British exports over the next few years.

There are other export measures in the check-list. My purpose in going through two in some detail is just to show the nature of the measures, that they are not just words, but are being worked out with great care and in great detail, that they are things which have not been done before and that they fit in at key points in the structure of the British export effort. In addition to these there is all the other work of BNEC, which has area committees now covering and able to advise in almost every major specialised market. There is even an area committee on a market as small as Israel. This is not just a proliferation of committees. Each market, as every exporter knows, is different and each needs a fund of specialised knowledge. There are the financial measures including the new export rebate and there is the work being done on exports in the little Neddies, which are now treating it as one of their priority subjects.

The final subject on the check-list under Balance of Payments is the Prices and Incomes Policy. I notice that everyone is now worried about the possible failure of the Incomes Policy, but it never was just an Incomes Policy. Prices are as much a part of the Policy as incomes, and, indeed, they are in the end the measure of its success. The best end for the country as a whole is a rise in productivity enabling wages to rise while prices remain stable. It is, therefore, vital that prices can be held until the rate of increase in money earnings begins to ease. If we can do this, then we will have a tremendous competitive edge over almost every other industrial country, none of which except

America has conquered the wage /price spiral. We shall also, in the short run, relieve the minds of those who have deposited £4,000M of liquid balances with us and, in the long run, introduce some equity into our social life between those who are dependent on fixed incomes and whose bargaining power is weak, and those whose bargaining power is temporarily strong. These aims are too important to be dropped with a weary shrug.

Of the remaining items on the check-list, I would single out investment in manufacturing as the most important. In the last five years manufacturing investment has increased most unevenly by 2·4% a year. This has got to go up to an increase of 7% a year, which we hope will be much steadier. We are certainly getting off to a good start. This is the only way in the long run to break our recurring balance of payments crises. We all know the past pattern. There is some increase in demand for a year or so; then domestic industry runs out of capacity and imports come in; then there is a credit squeeze to cut down demand; the importer is squeezed but so is the domestic producer and he restricts his investment in new capacity accordingly; then when demand is allowed to go ahead again, the shortage of domestic capacity is even more acute, the imports are even higher and the next squeeze on demand is tougher and longer; domestic industry once more marks down its investment intentions and so we might go on. The credit squeeze is only a short-run palliative. It does nothing constructive for the long term. It provides no way out.

The only way out in the long run is to make sure that capacity moves in step with demand and, if possible, a pace or so ahead. Extra capacity for exports must be created by increasing new investment not by restricting demand. Capacity to meet home demand from domestic production must be created by new investment and not by short-term squeezes on demand. In this period of the Plan, we must get off the vicious spiral and on to a virtuous spiral. Imports have a ratchet effect. They take the top of the demand curve when demand is going up, but they do not go away again when demand goes down. There is only one escape from the resulting severe switchback in demand for domestic producers and that is to see that imports do not get a hold in the first place. I believe many industries are much more aware of the dangers of trying to keep their plant utilisation up by letting imports take the peak of the demand curve and that this awareness of danger is one reason for the continued high rate of new investment. Continued investment is, therefore, not only right for the country, it is also good business, and the Government will continue to do its best to encourage new investment.

In addition, the Government will continue to encourage new investment by experienced companies from overseas, especially those whose exports to the UK already give them a level of sales on which they can base domestic production. This saves imports, increases investment and adds to the reserves all at one go. Investment from overseas has also, historically, been a tremendous help to the less developed areas of the country. It is often easier to persuade an American to go to Scotland than a Londoner! Indeed, it is hard to conceive of the picture in Ulster, Scotland and even the North-East without North American investment.

Finally, new investment is necessary to cover the manpower gap which the Plan has thrown up. At a 25% growth this is 400,000 and regional policies may reduce it to 200,000. But even if we bridge this gap, any growth in excess of 25% requires much better utilisation of labour. Nor is it just that there is a shortage of labour; what matters most is that it is a shortage of skilled labour. Here again the cycle of short-term credit squeezes has proved counter-productive in the long run. Demand has not been sustained for long enough to put pressure on those who are under-using skilled labour. Just when they are wondering whether they ought not to put in labour-saving machinery—for instance, numerically-controlled machine tools—they are suddenly taken off the hook by a down turn in demand. Instead of investing in modern plant they try to hold on to skilled labour which is under-utilised until demand is allowed to rise again. I get a little tired of metaphorical descriptions of the economy like 'over-heating'. But, to turn the metaphor on those who want us all cooled and deep-frozen, you must, in many industrial processes, use a great deal of heat to attain the critical temperature which turns useless material into a usable material. So often we have turned the heat off just before the critical point and the result is a complete waste of useful energy.

These are not inflationary policies. Quite the reverse. Inflation comes when demand exceeds supply. It is only a short-term solution to attain balance by reducing demand. In an age when people know that technology has made possible tremendous gains in material wealth for all, you cannot condemn the nation for ever to minute annual increases in national wealth. The only realistic way forward is to increase supply as fast or faster than demand. It is not realistic to suppose that demand can be somehow suppressed in the long run. This applies both to the supply of overall capacity and to the supply of new plant, which will save labour and especially scarce skilled labour. When supply comes up into line with demand we can achieve the financial stability which Britain must have both in the short and the long term.

The most important part of the Plan for industry is investment and I believe that to invest in Britain's industrial future is not only our patriotic duty but it is also good business.

The National Plan set out the need for more manufacturing investment and the need for industrial units which would be big enough to compete internationally. The Investment Grants and the IRC are two Government policies intended to help to achieve those aims, so I thought it appropriate to conclude the chapter on the Plan by a talk outlining the purposes of both policies.

Investment Grants

The new grants have to be paid for out of the total tax burden on industry and we cannot look just at their effect in giving relief on capital expenditure. Although free depreciation was the first choice of the CBI this would have put the cost to the

Government up by a very large sum—perhaps £300M a year or more.*

This would then have had to be raised by increased tax elsewhere and since companies would have benefited from free depreciation, there would have been a strong case for raising the extra tax on companies and not directly or indirectly on individuals. In discussions with the CBI it was, I think, generally agreed that free depreciation was not practical. Nor would a move to phased free depreciation have been any better. It would have spread the heavy cost over a number of years, but as an incentive it might well have been counter-productive, because companies might have been tempted to hold back investment until the maximum permitted write-off increased. Various other methods of obtaining the objectives of free depreciation were examined, but all were subject to the same sort of difficulty.

The desire to minimise the total burden of tax was also relevant to the argument that Corporation Tax 'devalued' the investment allowances by £100M, because the previous rate of tax on which they were allowed was $56\frac{1}{4}\%$ and Corporation Tax might be in the range of 35 to 40%. It would have been quite easy, without increasing the total overall burden of tax on industry, to raise the investment allowance *and* the rate of Corporation Tax in order to restore the £100M. This would discriminate much more heavily in favour of companies which invest and much more heavily against companies which do not. There is an argument for this if one is quite convinced that the investment allowance gives value for money as an incentive. But if it does not, then this puts a burden on the company which is not currently investing and does so to no very good purpose. If the grant is a better incentive, then it is not so necessary to try to recover £100M differential. This brings us to the arguments for and against going over to grants. In the replies to the CBI circular there was a slight margin in favour

---

* The CBI asked its members whether they preferred free depreciation, 15% grants, the existing system of investment allowances (which under Corporation Tax gave a lower rate of relief on capital expenditure) or a system of tax credits. Their first choice was for free depreciation by a substantial majority.

of the *status quo*. There was no means of knowing just why this was. It was not very large and could have been entirely accounted for by a feeling that grants were less certain than allowances. Industry's recent experience of grants is almost entirely of the grants made by the Board of Trade for investment in Development Areas. These are not given until the company has proved a case on grounds of additional employment and there is therefore considerable uncertainty until the case has been accepted. A grant payable on proof of expenditure on a qualifying item is, however, as certain as an investment allowance. Although there was, from the replies, evidence of much greater appreciation of discounted cash-flow techniques which enable a company to take the allowances into account in making investment decisions, I understand that some of the larger companies, and indeed one or two of the pioneers of discounted cash-flow, in fact favoured grants.

The great advantages of the grant as an incentive are its simplicity and its certainty. This is no doubt the reason why companies in the machine-tool industry and engineering industries have tended to favour grants.

Not everyone who has to decide whether to buy new plant, even in a large company, knows the company's likely cash-flow for ten years ahead or the company's tax position or the extent to which subventions from subsidiary or associated companies can look after their absence of taxable profits. Not every company accounting system gives credit for investment allowances in calculating the return on capital of a branch or subsidiary company. To the extent that those who made investment decisions were hazy as to the exact tax consequences, the investment allowances were ineffective. By contrast the grants are quite clear and the machine-tool salesman and the chief engineer with authority to spend up to £10,000 or £100,000 on replacement and improvement of his manufacturing equipment are both quite clear that the cost to the company will be only 80% or, in a Development Area, 60%.

The grant is not only simple, it is also certain. The purists are a little worried by this. They point out that the allowances only went to companies which made a profit and the grant goes to companies regardless of their profits. This, they maintain, will help to keep the inefficient companies in business and will encourage uneconomic investment. There are two answers to this. The first is that the grant is only a proportion of the investment. Four-fifths, or, in the case of the Development Areas three-fifths, still has to be found by the company from its own resources or on the market. The inefficient company which has no profits against which to set allowances is hardly likely to find it easy to raise the money it would need for its share of the investment. The market will see to that. No one is going to invest 80% of the needed finance in a dud company just because the Government is finding 20%. In practice it would need to find an even higher proportion. The amount needed for plant would almost certainly be doubled by the amount needed for stocks and debtors, not to mention investment qualifying at a lower rate such as buildings. I hardly think that the investment grants, useful though they are to an expanding company, are likely to send us off on a rake's progress of uneconomic investment by doubtful companies. The second answer to the purists is that with the ever increasing amount of investment needed for a given turnover—in the economic jargon, the tendency to higher capitalisation—there are an increasing number of companies whose annual allowances are swamped by investment allowances and who cannot therefore recover the full amount from taxable profits for several years. The grant will help them immediately.

Although the grant cannot at present be paid for eighteen months—which is the average delay on investment allowances —its certainty should be a real help in raising temporary finance on an investment.

The certainty also helps a great deal with the risks inevitable in new investment. When a board looks at a new project, it is above all conscious of the risks. However profitable and efficient a company, however assured it looks from the outside, every director knows that the future is uncertain. Past profits may look good to the market, but they are no assurance of future profits. Export markets may close, taste may change, overall demand may grow more slowly, there may be unexpected teething troubles with new and technically advanced equip-ment. At this point in time, when the risks of a projected invest-ment are uppermost, risks outside the control of even the best regulated business, it seems to me that a certain grant is more helpful than an allowance which is contingent on the early success of the investment. The one is a real insurance against inevitable risk, the other is only received if and when the risks fail to materialise. As an investment incentive, I think that the grant will therefore be more helpful. Admittedly the giant diversified multi-plant and multi-product company can cross-subsidise, but it can hardly be right to encourage diversification, some of which may be uneconomic, in order to enable firms to benefit from tax incentives to investment. The grants will give much more encouragement to the company whose resources are concentrated, especially the smaller specialised firm which is expanding fast. It will also give encouragement to the new over-seas investor, the kind of company which has been such a help in developing the economies of the Development Areas such as Northern Ireland and Scotland.

I would also like to say a word about discrimination. To the extent that the Corporation Tax does not differentiate so steeply as the previous system between those who invest and those who do not, the effect of discrimination on the total tax burden of a company is not so severe. There may be some people who think that it should be much more severe, but it is almost certainly better for industry to see how the new combination of Corporation Tax and Investment Grant work before doing anything more drastic. If the grants are as effective as they should be, heavy discrimination will be unnecessary and I imagine most businessmen would prefer to see how it works out first.

The line which the Government have drawn between those who will receive grants and those who will not is, very simply, between those areas of business which contribute directly and immediately to the import-export balance and those which do not. This is not a matter of Whitehall judgement. It is a matter of fact. In the long term, of course, everything contributes to a more efficient economy. In the long term higher investment in vehicles, in shops, in offices, in contractors' plant* all goes to make us more efficient.

But in the meantime what matters above all is the area of business which directly affects our balance of trade, because if that does not improve, we are not going to have the income to invest in anything else.

The balance of trade is affected immediately by manufacturing and shipping. Shipping, it goes without saying, contributes substantially to our invisible income. Our manufacturers export over a quarter of their total production. Other industries and services do earn currency, but the proportion to their total turnover is not nearly so high. We export getting on for £5,000M worth of goods a year and our costs internationally are competitive. But our share of world manufacturing capacity has been declining. All our industrial rivals have been putting down new capacity at a far higher rate than we have. Germany, for instance, has been investing over 30% more a year than we have.

As every businessman knows, it is very hard to keep your share of the market when your share of capacity declines. Your rivals can take on orders when you have to turn them down. New investment brings longer runs and lower costs. It brings technical improvements. But above all it enables you to keep your share of the business that is going. Our share in world trade has been declining. This trend must be reversed. We cannot afford a rush of imports every time we allow the economy to expand. We have the skill to make most of the manufactured and semi-manufactured goods we import and our labour costs are competititve. But our unit costs tend to rise because our production is held back by lack of capacity when that of our international competitors goes ahead at two or three times the rate of growth. Of course productivity is a matter of working harder, but in this day and age it is to a far greater extent a

---

* When the Selective Employment Tax was introduced, contractors, who had to pay it in full, were brought into the grants scheme to compensate. In choosing between the encouragement of exports and the encouragement of labour-saving, the Government had chosen the former, but the need for labour-saving investment in construction is very strong.

matter of having the plant. We need more industrial engineering and more hardware.

Of course you can make fun of discrimination. What is more important, says someone, more motorways or more plastic ducks? In the long run and in a social sense, perhaps motorways are more important. But I guarantee that we have imported more than a gross of plastic ducks in the last year and paid hard-earned currency to get them. The increase in consumer goods imports between 1963 and 1964 was about £50M. Unless we, a trading nation, are going to erect barriers to international trade on top of those which already exist or unless we are to tell our children that they can have no more toys until the balance of payments problem has been solved, then toys are going to be a factor in the import-export balance. And after all the balance of payments problem is not the fault of the five-year-old.

Manufacturing is the pace-setter for the economy. The rest of the economy, services, banking, distribution, catering, will not prosper and expand unless manufacturing expands. You cannot have a strong banking business, for instance, on a weak manufacturing base, and manufacturing will not expand without a higher rate of investment, a rate which allows us to meet rising domestic demand without a disproportionate rise in imports and a rate which allows us to keep and expand our share in world trade.

Industrial Re-organisation Corporation

I thought that you might also like to have some comments on the second White Paper just published in the IRC. A glance at the Fortune list of major international companies demonstrates vividly that although British industry has its giants like Shell, Unilever and ICI, it does not, in general, field companies of comparable size with those in USA and, in some key industries, German and Japanese companies have an uncomfortable edge in the scale of their operations. Even some Swiss and Dutch companies are bigger than their British opposite numbers. There does also seem to be a tendency on the part of many

British companies to diversify rather than to concentrate, so that the unit of operation, even in a large British company, can be smaller than the company's size would seem to indicate.

There are, of course, industries where size does not matter, though they are becoming fewer. But even in an industry where there is still plenty of room for the small company, it is usually necessary to have a number of large companies who are the technical pace-setters and to whom the rest of the industry may be suppliers and sub-contractors. However, in most technically advanced industries, scale of operations is essential. America's population is almost four times ours and their income per head is two and a half times ours, so their total market is getting on for ten times our market. An American company with the same market share as its British equivalent would therefore be ten times its size. This means, not just a stepping up of the quantity of research and development it can do, but a stepping up of the whole scope and quality. It is a completely different kind of operation. The whole process of technical innovation can be speeded up. Half a dozen projects can go forward where the British company can only carry one. There are, therefore, six times the chances of a technical breakthrough. The bigger company will be test-marketing while the smaller is still wondering whether its idea will work out at all. In technical back-up in export markets, the bigger company will always have the edge. This can command a premium in price of anything from 5% upwards. But there may come a day when only the technically advanced product will sell at all. Now in theory we can let the market look after all this, but there are two things to remember about the market. First, the market knows no frontiers and secondly, advances in technology are so swift today and so decisive, that if you are beaten in the market, there is no comeback. You cannot catch up again on an international rival whose inbuilt rate of technological advance is several times as swift as your own. Success breeds success and to fall behind is to be killed stone dead. That is the way the market works and the market is not going to look after just us because we are British.

Of course we could, if we fell behind, rely on buying our

technology from foreigners and many smaller countries have done this in the past. But if we must sell over a third of our manufacturing production in world markets—and we must—and if our absolute volume must remain the second or third highest in the world—and it must—it is not really open to us to rely on foreign technology or to specialise like Sweden, Switzerland, Holland or Belgium. We must stay in the race alongside the leaders.

Otherwise we will find the foreign parent company, the foreign licensor increasingly under pressure from his home sales force, let alone his export salesmen, to give his major customers a two to three-year technological lead on any advance which really matters. Since the British subsidiary, associate or licensee, will probably yield a revenue which is only a fraction of that of the big domestic customer, this pressure is unlikely to be resisted. The buying power of the big battalions is there and we have to keep up with it.

There is room for argument as to whether the present institutions in the City are enough to see that we obtain the concentration we need and that we have it fast enough. The City already puts through a very high volume of mergers and it can be argued that it will not turn away any merger which is likely to be profitable. However, the job of IRC will not be quite the same as the job of a merchant bank. As one banker said to me, 'I have my time cut out merging clients who come to me wanting to be merged and I don't have time to go round persuading people who have not thought of it'. Another said to me 'We've got half a dozen big jobs going through the shop and those have to carry the projects which are just at talking stage, so we can't afford to spend too much time just talking'. The job of IRC will be to find and talk to the people who might want to be merged and to come to the merchant banks when some of the talking is over, when the project has turned from a possible into a probable. It will therefore provide an advance screen for the City which should be entirely helpful and complementary to the work in which the City is so skilled.

CHAPTER TEN

Micro-economics — the Little Neddies

The first speech on the Economic Development Committees was given to the Institute of Builders at their annual meeting in April 1965 just as they were about to set up their own committee. Since it was mainly an outline of objectives, I have included a further speech on the actual work of the Economic Development Committees which was given to the London Graduate School of Business Studies almost a year later in 1966.

The speech to the Builders was politely received. They assured me that though they did not feel that they could judge the usefulness of little Neddies, they were most impressed by the sincerity of my own belief that they were worthwhile and would be very glad to have a go, which they subsequently did. The London Business School was an audience more professional in the machinery of Government and in macro and micro-economics and there was some brisk cross-questioning, especially from the academic staff. Perhaps the fact that the Principal was a member of the Electrical Engineering EDC made them more sympathetic than they might have been, but they seemed prepared to be persuaded.

I do believe that there is a real need for institutional machinery for the reconciliation of the public interest with the private interests of capital and labour, a need for some flexible supervision of the market economy and above all a need of some gearing down process through which the macro-economics of the national economy can be meshed with the micro-economics of each industry and company. The EDCs may or may not be the right instrument for these operations. If they are not, then another will no doubt be found. But at the very least they are a beginning and a hopeful beginning too.

To a great extent these talks are based on hope rather than on achievement, on what might be done rather than on what has been done. When the last talk was given, the older EDCs had only been going for two years and half of the EDCs had only been alive for a matter of months. It takes time and hard work, trial and experiment, for a new institution

139

to find its place and try its strength. Since I gave these talks, explaining all that EDCs can do, I have been appointed Director General of NEDC and since the EDCs are now one of my primary responsibilities I will now have to put into practice what I have been preaching.

The functions of EDCs were laid down in 1963 as being the improvement of the economic performance of the industry and the provision of information on prospects and plans for the industry in relation to national growth objectives. These seem straightforward enough, but in fact it was quite a break with traditional Government-industry relations. Until then, Government had relied on the competitive mechanism of the market economy governed only by regulation of demand and general legislation on monopoly, restrictive trade practices and company accounting. But it was a necessary recognition that, in an economy as dependent as we are on the balance of trade, the only way of ensuring the expansion of demand is to ensure the expansion of supply. Otherwise, the demand regulator can only be moved to 'dead slow' between intervals at 'stop'. A lot of people think of course that any interference with the competitive market economy is wrong, that the market economy is somehow natural and that anything else is highly unnatural — conveniently ignoring the fact that the market economy in a highly industrialised country is, itself, artificial and has to have a whole body of complicated legislation to enable it to work at all. And given the choice, I would sooner the affairs of my industry were in the hands of a committee of living men, than regulated in this rapidly-changing world solely by the dead hand of legislation.

In fact, however, the EDCs and the market economy can work hand in hand together. The market economy is a very useful instrument to move resources of man and capital from the inefficient units to the efficient and in an economy of the size of the United States — six or seven times our size — this may be enough, but in a smaller economy such as ours so heavily dependent upon overseas trade, there is a place for co-operation as well as competition. This is something which the businessman often understands better than the academic economist.

Economic theory would put the inefficient company to the wall, but the inefficient company often takes an unconscionable long time a-dying and it is, in any case, questionable whether an investment in men and physical resources in major companies today is now so great that we cannot afford the spectacle of a large company slowly moving downhill in the hands of faltering management. We ought to have a system to make sure that its resources are put to best use long before the final break-up and redundancy. But desirable as this may be, are the Economic Development Committees the kind of bodies which can help? Are they, without sanctions, relying largely on goodwill and co-operation, just another do-good institution to produce fractionally better results, or are they effective bodies capable of making a major breakthrough in national productivity? I firmly believe they can be a very considerable factor in the national economy.

The EDCs will work best where the market economy alone does not give the results required for rapid and sustained economic growth or does not give them fast enough. For instance, exports are profitable enough to give us a total volume of over £4,500M, but we need a further £500M and in this marginal area a company may find that the market economy alone guides it to take home orders to preserve its share of home business from competitors. Export delivery dates may begin to affect home delivery dates. Yet it is not in our competitors' real interests that the industry should be unable to exploit its foreign markets to the full, since this limits Britain's own expansion which, in turn, affects the size of their home market. I hope, therefore, that it may not be impossible to devise methods which must vary from industry to industry, but which will have the effect of increasing the industry's capacity for export.*

No less important to the trade balance are imports. Here the problem is slightly different. No one wants to prevent freer international trade. As a major trading nation we depend on trade freedom from tariffs and other restrictions. But the

* A number of EDCs have shown an interest in the possibility of setting up an Export Corporation for their industry. This however is only one of several means which might be adopted.

volume of imports is so large that there must be many imports we could make as economically ourselves and without damaging the volume of international trade. To get out of our reliance on imports we need not only a greater increase in exports, but a substantial improvement in UK manufacturing capacity. Contact between customer and supplier EDCs can be most helpful here. It is to be hoped that this work between EDCs will mean that, as the output of the industry grows, the output of its suppliers will keep pace and that there will be no need to depend on foreign imports of materials which can be made well and cheaply here.

Another major task which it is thought most EDCs can tackle with profit is the standardisation of the industry's products. This sounds a very mundane subject, not one to set the Thames on fire, yet there is evidence that attention to this alone could produce a real industrial breakthrough. What we need in the short run is more capacity with the same plant and labour-force. We need this for added exports and we need it to expand without the crippling burden of imports. In the long run, extra capacity can give us more output per man, but in the short run we can only get it from standardisation. All my business experience tells me that the gains are great and there are weighty reasons for thinking that the market economy alone will not give them, at any rate, in the short run.

One quick guide to the potential standardisation available is to discover how many hours of the weekly total of 168 a piece of plant is actually working. I remember, when we worked a big opencast dragline, watching this figure each week. I think it cost us a pound a second to have the machine idle and this cost of not working is well worth computing. I feel sure that there are a good many plants in Britain where machines are actually operating for only 20 to 30% of the time available. Now I am not suggesting that a piece of equipment should work 100% — that would be clearly impossible — but there are, I believe, great areas of industry where, given reasonable product standardisation, output could be increased by up to half as much again improving utilisation from say 30 to 45%. Furthermore, mass production of standard parts normally helps to achieve much greater consistency with better yields and fewer inspection delays and expensive remakes.

Now, how does it come about that the market economy does not sort this out. I heard of a company the other day which did custom dyeing and with every change of dye the vat had to be emptied, cleaned and filled. One of their customers made corsets and his customers apparently demanded for their corsets forty-five shades of pink. Well, I know that ladies' fashion was not, perhaps, the best subject for standardisation, but this struck me as the limit! Why, the friend who told me the story asked, did he not charge less for five standard shades and much more for the remaining forty? Well, this, he said, would upset the customer who wanted his forty-five shades and if he did not get them at the standard price he would go somewhere else.

This is not the only man in Britain who will not change an illogical price structure. Once a price structure is accepted, businessmen are reluctant to change it, lest they unleash a price war. Personally, I think that this is more likely in the long run to do damage to the industry, since illogically high prices eventually lead to excess capacity or substitution, but a lot of people are tempted to hope that the long run will look after itself. So they go on in a jobbing business at high prices while they could produce 50% more at lower prices, until the long run runs out and an importer making nothing but standards for overseas markets, begins to pick out all the plums in their market and leaves them to make nothing but the lines which create all the costs and overheads. I once worked out in a particular case that 80% of the overhead was caused by 15% of the volume and that 85% of the volume could therefore be manufactured for only 20% of the overhead.

It is our hope that the Economic Development Committees can get suppliers and customers together and can get them to sort out the lines which the market really needs and those which it could do without, taking into account the increased output and lower costs which would be available if the industry's plant were run on standard products without the interruption of expensive specials and non-standards. I must mention that standardisation of component parts does not mean a lack of variety in the final product; it normally means a much better final product.

These are three examples of the kind of task which the EDCs can tackle and which are complementary to the function of the market economy. But they are by no means the only tasks. The DEA is responsible for the National Economic Plan. In this mammoth task it is essential that the figures and assumptions for the whole economy shall be based on the best possible information in each industry. Each industry has its own problems and many of them are very far from the national average. No one pretends that the sum total of the information given to the DEA is likely to be right to three places of decimals, but at least Government in doing its planning should know what industry's own plans are, should know the assumptions on which those plans are based and should have a convenient forum in which to discuss them with the industry. It is much more helpful to do this in a forum where the participants meet regularly, where they know each other's problems and aims and where there is mutual trust and respect, than in a meeting of virtual strangers who meet for this purpose only.

The Plan does not solve every problem, but increasing capital investment needed by industry makes it most desirable to do all that is possible to reduce the uncertainty and risk in new investment. Risk is inevitable in business, but there is no need to clasp it to our bosom! If it can in any way be minimised by greater information on the estimated demand of our customer industries, then let us do all we can to minimise it. The authorisation of great capital schemes is a heavy responsibility and we should have all the information we can get. We will not arrive in the ideal world at once, but the planning process should help to throw up the likely bottlenecks in good time and since it now needs anything up to two or three years to create additional capacity in some industry, we need much more advance warning of these bottlenecks than we did when the whole industrial process was simpler.

The EDCs can, I hope, do work in future in areas where it is not worth while for one company to act, but where action is necessary collectively to safeguard the future of the industry.

It may be said that all this can be done within the normal relationship between a Trade Association and the sponsor department. However, my own experience of these relationships as an industrialist is that they are rather more intermittent, than the relationships in an EDC. Government policy very often has to be secret until it is decided—the budget is only one example—and very often the industry does not know there is a case to be made and the Government does not know that there are unseen implications, in the policy until it is all water under the bridge. There is no substitute for keeping Government continuously in the picture on the major problems in the industry. The DEA is a policy department rather than an executive department. It is interested in the sound growth of the whole economy and cannot be held to be an interested party in the case of any part of the economy or any particular aspect of economic policy. Its participation in the EDC as well as the participation of the sponsoring department can lend the more weight to any proposals for Government action when these come to be discussed in Whitehall and in Cabinet.

All the EDCs are constitutionally related through the National Economic Development Council and Office and this relationship has already proved to be a most useful channel of communication between industries. In theory, the selling industry and the buying industry should know what the other is up to. It is remarkable how many gaps have to be filled by direct communication between EDCs. Neither the machinery of Government Departments nor of industry fulfils this function quite so well as the NEDC machinery.

Last, but most important, the unions are very rarely represented on the normal machinery of Government/industry consultation, but they play their full part in the EDC. In my view, union participation in industrial policy is both right and necessary, and it seems to me that this is the right level at which they should participate. They must of course participate at national level and here the TUC do play a very full part; but to leave it at that would be to risk a feeling of remoteness on the part of the ordinary union member from the decision making process. Experiments in bringing unions in at Company level have not been very successful. However at industry level on the EDCs we have in Britain some very able unionists who can play a full part in the discussion and are fully involved in the problems and opportunities of the industry.

However this is theory. What matters is practice. It is early days yet in the history of a very new national institution, but I know that these little Neddies are mostly lively bodies, full of vigorous argument. If I read a newspaper headline 'Row on little Neddy' it does not worry me any more than 'row in the House' worries a politician. What both indicate is that the institution is alive and kicking and that the people attending think that what is decided there matters enough to be worth an argument. I am reminded of a story of a tutor of mine at Cambridge, who was parachuted into a small European country whose language he spoke well, to help the resistance. Unfortunately he found that there were two resistances intent on firing off at each other all the ammunition which had been so dangerously flown out to them. At great personal hazard he got them round a table in a remote farmhouse. While there was vigorous argument with everyone shouting and pounding the table he felt that there was hope, but suddenly they all became very calm and terribly quiet and polite and treated each other with the most elaborate courtesy. He realised sadly that the end had come and that they had fallen out irrevocably; there was nothing more to be done and sure enough next morning there they were shooting at each other again well out of range until they wasted all the ammunition. But although there is argument in plenty, it is constructive, a lot of high hurdles have already been overcome and the proposals for action coming out now from all the EDCs are realistic and practical and likely, in my view, even in the limited field so far covered to produce far reaching and beneficial changes in British industry.

. . .

The National Economic Development Council is different from any other previous bodies charged with advising Government or consulting with Government on economic or industrial matters. Its difference lies in its own access to the grass roots of industry through the Economic Development Committees. All previous national bodies have been no more authoritative than the sum of the high level personages round the table. Lord This and Sir John That could give their views—and did. But, in fact, their views were often narrowly based, coming overwhelmingly from one section of one industry and as often as not founded on experience which was in danger of being a little out of date. I have read the minutes of such meetings and it is small wonder that they cut such little ice with Government or that the various do-good committees were regarded by business as a job to keep Uncle Harry out of mischief and not as an opportunity to get something done.

Business may seem simple to the tycoon who knows his customers, his labour force and his technology, but looked at from a national point of view it is incredibly complex. We now have twenty EDCs and the probability is that there will, in the end, be twenty-five and that will not cover the whole of industry. Not only is each industry quite different from every other industry, but it has been quite a task to persuade branches of the same industry that they have enough in common to serve in the same EDC. I know that in the Aluminium industry it was hard to persuade us that we had much in common with the Copper boys. As for Lead and Zinc, we never even thought about them. Yet the total employment in non-ferrous metals is hardly enough to justify a separate EDC.

It is the job of the NEDC to establish a base of agreed facts through the EDCs. Up to now this factual base has usually been confined to industries in immediate trouble, and even then the information has been patchy. But soundly based information is more needed than it ever has been before. Industry has never before been carried on on today's scale and complexity. Indeed, industry as we now know it is a relatively new phenomenon, almost a post-war phenomenon. We have to find some way by which it can fit into the machinery of Government and the process of making national economic decisions. We have inherited this machinery and these processes from generations which had quite different problems and quite different time scales. There used to be less inter-dependence between Government and industry and we used not to live on the same knife-edge in this country between success and disaster. But, more important, we had lower economic expectations. Everyone today knows of the growth of science and technology and this generation is not going to tolerate a Government which cannot find a way of tapping these boundless new sources of wealth. My own view is that this generation is right, though we must not lose our liberty in the process. We must therefore have new machinery and this must fit into the context of a free society. The EDCs are voluntary bodies and must remain so, but they are capable of establishing the facts of life for their industry. They are a forum in which the improvement of the economic performance of the industry can not only be discussed but firm proposals can be made to the constituent bodies, Government, management and unions about the part each can play in bringing this improved performance about. Planning is not just a statistical exercise. If action does not result from the information, then the whole exercise is barren.

How has this new machinery been found to work in practice and what results have been achieved?

One of the bigger efforts of the EDCs so far has been their part in the preparation of the National Plan published in October 1965. I have circulated a list of EDCs showing when they were set up, the numbers employed in the industries which they cover and a note of their chairmen.

The consultations with industry were carried out in two stages. In the first stage industries were asked to provide estimates of their output, exports, employment and investment needs in 1970 on the basis of 25% growth; and also to give their assessment of the conditions necessary for the realisation of these estimates. In the second stage meetings were held with representatives of NEDO (the Office serving the Council and Government Departments at which the industry answers were reviewed in comparison with the aggregate estimates and so far as possible with replies received from other industries). Industries were asked first to estimate demand for their products at home and abroad (and the proportion of the home market held by imports) in 1970 on the 25% growth assumption. An indication was also required of the extent of revision of present plans that would be needed for this demand to be met. Ideally, industries might have been asked to provide for comparison an estimate of the sum of firms' plans for output in 1970.

Similar questions were asked about investment and labour requirements to meet the 1970 output estimates, and firms' present expectations. A distinction was drawn between definite commitments to expenditure and expectations. They were asked for separate estimates of qualified and skilled employees and for any expected shortages. Industries were asked to split their estimates of employment and investment between the regions, and where they foresaw shortages of particular types of labour, to indicate in which regions they were expected.

Finally, they were asked to indicate the extent of the possibilities of an immediate increase in labour productivity without additional investment and to comment on the action required for the achievement of the 1970 estimates they had provided. The estimates for each industry were then discussed by the appropriate EDC; in a number of cases they were amended; and in each case the EDC commented on their implications. The detailed estimates were prepared with the aid of the Input/Output Model from the Cambridge Social Accounting Matrix.

As soon as the preliminary replies were received they were added up, with estimates for uncovered sectors, to give national totals of output, exports, investment and employment in 1970. The results showed a total increase in output of nearly 25%, but a significant excess in the demand for labour over the expected supply. The industries were estimating a large increase in exports. The investment estimates for manufacturing industry in 1970 seemed less than adequate.

The industry estimates of output were also compared with the estimates of demand on each industry in 1970 which had been obtained using the SAM Input/Output Model. This is based on a table showing, for each of thirty-one industry sectors, its total output (in 1960), the input of materials, fuels and purchased services required for that output from each other industry and its requirements of imports. It also shows how much of an industry's output goes to other industries as their raw materials, how much to private and public consumption and investment and how much to exports. Estimates can be made of the way the input structure of each industry will have changed by 1970, and estimates of final demand in that year can then be turned back into estimates of total demand on each industry, including the demands made on it by other industries which use its products as their materials. For example, demand for cars results in car production, which itself throws demand on, for instance, the steel and rubber industries, and through them on practically all other industries. This demand will of course create further demand on the motor industry itself.

The estimates were discussed with industry representatives in the 'dialogue' meetings, which took place in EDCs or at meetings arranged for the purpose by NEDO or the Departments concerned. They provided an occasion for industry representatives to explain and discuss the difficulties they expected to experience in fulfilling their output and export estimates for 1970 and the action by them, by other industries and by the Government required to overcome them.

In the course of the dialogues a large number of revisions were nevertheless made, both to the industry estimates and to the general estimates, in the direction of improving consistency.

The initial estimates of exports made by industries were, as mentioned, rather surprisingly high. They implied a total increase at a rate of $5\frac{1}{2}\%$ in volume per annum, slightly more than was needed (given the effect of policies on other items) to meet the balance of payments objective, and much faster than over the last decade.

At the conclusion of the dialogues, 'annexes' to the published National Plan were prepared for each industry, setting out the 1970 estimates resulting from the Industrial Inquiry, as amended in the course of the 'dialogue' and commenting on them. These annexes were agreed with representatives of the industry concerned, including the trade unions.

The first nine EDCs were set up in 1964 and for the next year the detailed work on the Plan absorbed a good deal of their time and energy. The next five EDCs were not set up until the Summer of 1965 and a further six were set up right at the end of 1965. For the work of the Plan, therefore, we must rely mainly on the experience of the first nine, and in their work the Plan has taken time and effort. This was not quite the first time this had been tried. There was the 1963 NEDC Plan. The EDCs were not then in existence but NEDO had approached the Trade Associations and had established the contacts from which sprang the first nine EDCs. There had, therefore, been a first run, though not on quite such an ambitious scale. The 1965 Plan represented a major step forward, but although it was much better than anything which had gone before, it is still pretty rough by comparison with what should be possible in the next major exercise. Too few companies take a five year look, too few industries are accustomed to putting their collective heads together and we have too little experience of the weight we need to give to the variables, of the effect of the variables on each other, of the effect of macro-economic decisions on micro-economic decisions.

We need much greater understanding of the underlying forces behind micro-economic decisions. Who really hoards labour and why? How effective are the forces of competition? To what extent is wage pressure a result of market forces and to what extent is it a result of traditional annual wage negotiation, the stately institutional minuet, led off by union A and ending up, in due order, at the close of the round by union Z?

We can freeze the economic picture at the moment of time and see for instance how it looks now or give our current estimate of the view five years ahead, rather like those models of the Battle of Waterloo at critical points in the action. But just as the old Duke could not be persuaded to look at a model of the battle or read an account of it, because his memory of the battle was dynamic, something which never stopped but went on and on in bloody din and confusion, so some participants in the confused industrial struggle do not find a static model useful because they know that in real life nothing stands still. Certainly what we need in the end is a dynamic model but we can only get that if we start off with the basic data at a moment of time and see how it works out over a period.

The Government are planning to publish a progress report in the Autumn of 1966. This will not contain a full statement on each industry, it will comment on a number of key industrial sectors. Before then they will be discussing the Plan figures for their industry with a representative expert group from each EDC and this will include union representatives. Although it is undesirable at the present stage of skill to do a major revision of the whole Plan each year, some industries may wish to revise figures which they gave last year and we may wish to come forward with rather more detailed input/output analyses than on the last occasion, for discussion with the industries concerned.

The second and more dynamic function of the EDCs is to improve the economic performance of their industry. Each industry has its own range of problems and opportunities, but there have been a number of problems which because of their national importance have been tackled across the board. Almost all of the EDCs have done major studies on imports and exports as they affect their own industry and a number are now turning to work on improving the use of resources in their industries, both in skills and manpower and in capital equipment.

While the action recommended by the EDC to the Government results in firm executive action, action recommended to industry has to be left to individual companies and unions. Government action can be seen and, to some extent, measured. Industrial decisions are made behind closed doors and only emerge intermittently into view. What is going on can, therefore, only be guessed and for that reason, the total sum can never be measured. This is as it should be in a free society, but it makes it peculiarly hard for those of us who have to say what the EDCs have, in their short careers, actually done to improve the economic performance of their industries. It could be that they are no more than another series of talking shops, but my own view is that they are, in fact, having considerable effect and will have an even stronger effect once they really get established. By 1968 when they will all have a couple of years behind them and some will have had four, they will have found out where to put their weight, and they will certainly have discovered by trial and error the key spots in their industry which really make the difference to their performance.

The job of persuading a whole industry, controlled in the main by the old hands who have been brought up in it, to change their ways because a committee says so, sounds an undertaking so formidable that a lot of people might be inclined to write it off from the start. However, that is not the way it works. In every industry there are the pace-setters and the laggards, with a greater or lesser number of firms in between who are not as good as they might be, but are ready to be convinced if a good case is put to them. The real laggards no one will ever convince. My friends in the management consultancy profession tell me that they avoid them if they possibly can. The result, they feel, is not just worth the effort. They concentrate, if they can, on the leaders and on those who are prepared to follow. This is where the real advances can be made.

The EDC combines, to some extent, the functions of a Royal Commission and a propagandist body. It has the advantage over a Royal Commission that it is in constant session. Members of Royal Commissions have been known to complain that at the crucial point, when something begins to be done, they are firmly wound up and sent home. They have no means of saying that that was *not* what they meant. They have to sit frustrated while their wisdom is misapplied or while the inactivists argue that it has all been overtaken by events. They cannot advise an altered mixture if the first does not work. Above all, they do not have a propaganda function beyond the covers of the blue book. Yet the broad course of British life has been altered very largely by the contents of those blue books. These become the basic facts on which decisions are made.

If EDCs were recommending less profitable action to their industry, one would not expect them to have much effect. But they are recommending action to promote economic development which is by its nature profitable. It may be that there are companies where managerial lethargy predominates over the desire to improve profitability, even over the desire for long term survival; but the EDCs are working with the forces of the market economy and not against them and they are speaking to a wider audience than company directors. They are speaking to customers, to investors, to Government, to union leaders, not to mention all the other people for whose good esteem the industry and the individual industrialist really care—including their potential recruits and even their personal friends. On the whole people want to work in a progressive industry and not in one whose best friends must regard it as backward. For all these reasons, I believe that what is said by the EDCs matters and will matter even more in the future.

Given that it is hard to measure exactly the effect of an EDC in its industry because so much of it is not visible, is there any result which is visible, any token tip of the iceberg?

One EDC where the results are somewhat more in the open because of the nature of the decisions which have to be taken is the EDC for the Movement of Exports, chaired by Lord Caldecote. The object of this EDC was to see if we could move from the nineteenth-century dock system to a system which used all the modern means of transport between the British factory and the foreign customer. The EDC brought together, for the first time, all the providers of the services *en route* with all the users of those services. No one of the users' interests had enough buying power to change the pattern of transport and no one of the providers could, on his own, change the pattern because he was dependent on what came before and what went after on the route. One of the objects of the exercise was to cut down the overall time needed to move exports. Another was to improve the reliability of delivery dates. The EDC declared its interest in roll-on roll-off ferries, in container freight, in inland clearance depots in major industrial centres so that customs could give clearance to container freight well away from the clutter of dock areas. It also declared an interest in air freight.

Before it was set up, I had the greatest difficulty in persuading people that these new methods held the key to the future in the movement of freight. But now, though the EDC has been going for not much over half a year, not only are these all a matter of common talk, but two major consortia have been set up by shipping groups, each proposing to integrate backwards and own their own haulier companies and each proposing to set up inland clearance depots. Two major sites have already been bought and I believe that others are under negotiation. Both roll-on roll-off and air freight increased substantially in the last year and both British Rail and Scandinavian lines have commissioned more roll-on roll-off ferries. In 1964 exports to Europe, excluding fuel, were £157M; of this 13% went by air, 8% by roll-on roll-off, 5% by train ferry and 74% by conventional ship. The latter includes some container traffic.

Even the longest haul is now more economic by container because the dramatic cut in turn-round time greatly increases the availability of the ships which spend their time at sea and not in the dock. A year ago I could find no one who could tell me these economics. (This may have been my fault, but they certainly did not seem widely known.) Since then a number of the major shipping groups have done some intensive study and I have been told that they have, as a result of this, greatly accelerated their plans for moving over to the use of containers. Meantime, the EDC is going forward with a major study of the time taken for goods to move to Europe. It has been found that the average time is about ten days but there is a tail where the time taken is up to twenty or thirty days. The study will try to discover how much the shortening of this tail, apart from the lowering of the overall time, would be a factor with continental customers and how far the increased dependability of delivery would increase their likelihood of buying British.

The first major study undertaken by most of the EDCs was on imports. The results of these studies for the first nine EDCs were brought together in the NEDC paper on Imported Manufactures which was published last year. This has had wide repercussions both in industry and has also affected Government policy. One of the major reasons for the increase in imports has been shortage of capacity in British industry. Most industries now seem determined that the next major move forward in the economy is not going to find them short of capacity as the last one did. This can be seen most dramatically

in industries such as chemicals where there has been a rapid up-
surge in new capacity and where there are continual studies
on the imported chemicals to establish which of them should be
manufactured in the UK. It can also be seen, I believe, in the
continued strength of industrial investment, particularly investment in plant and machinery which has gone at a much
higher rate than in previous investment cycles. Even if there
is now some levelling off, the overall total will still almost
certainly be better.

Another result of the import study has been a series of maker-
user consultations, especially in mechanical engineering. This
has arisen from the enquiries carried out among the industry's
customers to find out why they bought foreign machines.
There have been maker-user meetings in chemical plant leading
to a joint study on demand for plant and on the ordering of
foreign plant. There have been maker-user meetings in textile
machinery, leading to a joint study of the technical performance
of some imported looms. There has been a third maker-user
meeting in the Chocolate and Confectionery EDC, leading to a
new interest in their requirements by a major British engineerng
company. A fourth group has been started between makers,
users and research laboratories to do joint research on die-
casting machines. Sometimes the stories coming out of these
confrontations can be quite dramatic. One supplier swore
that his sales engineers were in 'constant' touch with a particular customer who, in turn, swore that they never darkened
his door. A little investigation showed that the last time any
representative of the company had visited them was thirteen
years before!

In addition to these confrontations, groups of companies have
got together to rationalise their production of particular lines
and the British Chemical Contractors Association has been
formed to help to set up consortia to tackle large chemical
installations.

Another important EDC among the first nine is electrical
engineering. As well as the general studies on imports and
exports, it has had a number of projects of its own. It has given
considerable stimulus to the adoption of metric standards.

It has set up a working party with the Ministry of Power on standardisation and variety reduction. One of the most dramatic results here has been a reduction in the variety of cables required by CEGB and Area Boards from 250 to about 25. It also has a working party on the rationalisation of production which has been studying the economies of scale in production and marketing of distribution transformers. The Electricity Supply Authorities and the industry now meet regularly to see how the Authorities can help the industry in their efforts on exports and in improving their general economic performance. The EDC has studied two reports by consultants on imports, one on the import of foreign domestic electric appliances coming from the Distribution EDC (which has also helped other EDCs in this way) and another on imports of industrial electric equipment which has been undertaken by an outside consultant. The EDC has invited the industry to make statistical returns on investment, labour and other key data so that the background of facts on which decisions can be taken in the industry and outside should be greatly improved. The Customs and Excise have also agreed to make material improvements in the published figures on imports.

All the EDCs have also been undertaking a major study on exports. Most of them have so far only been able to put in interim reports, but already a certain pattern is emerging. Very few EDCs seem to find capacity a limiting factor in expanding their exports. All wholeheartedly approve of the setting up of the EDC for the Movement of Exports. None of the EDCs seem to think that pick-a-back schemes have much chance of success, but many are interested in an Export Corporation to buy as a principal from British Manufacturers and to sell overseas through the Corporation's own marketing and sales organisation. This would be especially helpful with consumer goods. In capital goods it was thought that consortia might be more helpful.

One could go on outlining the activities of each EDC and the conclusions on one subject after another. Perhaps this is enough to show the variety of work which is going on. The improvement in economic performance we need is marginal.

The EDCs are not asked to do miracles, just to get a marginal improvement in investment, in exports and in productivity. We might get these improvements without them, but with them I think we will surely succeed.

Addendum

The debate in the House of Lords on the Plowden Committee Report on the aircraft industry gave some revealing insights into the limitations of outside *ad hoc* committees. Lord Plowden's own speech was particularly interesting and it is worth quoting one extract.

'I should now like to touch on the whole question of how problems such as the one put to our Committee should be dealt with. I do not think that an *ad hoc* Committee such as ours is the right way. The members of our Committee were largely ignorant of the industry when we were appointed. This was deliberate. We were chosen as a "jury" —a body of men without preconceptions or already fixed positions on the subjects we were investigating. We were extremely short of time and pressed against our better judgement to report in less than a year after we were appointed. This meant that most of our time was absorbed by taking evidence and learning the basic facts. Even two more months would probably have doubled our "thinking" time, and the paradox is that, just as we were reaching some understanding of the problems of the industry, we finished our report and the Committee disbanded. The expertise, so painstakingly and expensively acquired, is unlikely ever to be used again ... How much more sensible it would have been to have had this job done by a Standing Committee ... a Committee with a strong permanent secretariat charged with the continued study of the problems involved ...'*

* House of Lords 'Official Report', Tuesday, 1st March 1966, cols 618 and 619.

FORMATION OF EDCs

Date of Formation Meeting	Industry	Number employed June 1964	Chairman
April 1964	Machine Tools ..	88	Sir Stewart Mitchell
April 1964	Chemicals	456	Mr G. N. Beeby
April 1964	Electronics	295	Sir Donald Stokes
May 1964	Chocolate & Sugar Confectionery ..	95	Sir Joseph Latham
May 1964	Paper and Board	97	Sir Thomas Robson
May 1964	Mechanical Engineering ..	1,192	Mr D. A. C. Dewdney
May 1964	Wool Textiles ..	187	Mr Mosley Isle
May 1964	Electrical Engineering ..	509	Sir Leslie Robinson
July 1964	Distributive Trades	3,151	Sir Hugh Weeks
June 1965	Building	2,088 ⎫	Lord Campbell
June 1965	Civil Engineering	⎬	
June 1965	Movement of Exports	—	Lord Caldecote
June 1965	Food Processing	526	Sir Joseph Latham
June 1965	Rubber	130	Mr J. E. Bolton
Nov 1965	Hotels and Catering	731	Mr William Swallow
Dec 1965	Newspaper, Printing and Publishing	391	Mr H. R. Mathys
Dec 1965	Post Office	419	Sir Andrew Crichton
Dec 1965	Clothing	448	Mr Robert Appelby
Dec 1965	Hosiery and Knitwear	128	Mr David Nicholson
Dec 1965	Agriculture	900	*

* A chairman is still to be established for this EDC.

CHAPTER ELEVEN

The Policy for Productivity, Prices and Incomes

The two following speeches cover the policy for productivity, prices and incomes. The first speech, given to the Bristol Chamber of Commerce in the Spring of 1965 is on prices and incomes and the second, to the trades union research officers at TUC headquarters is on productivity.

At the moment of writing it seems that the policy has been fairly successful in damping down prices. Productivity growth since the board was set up a year ago has been slightly below average and the increase in incomes, on any count, has been a good deal higher than average. I have pointed out in the first speech that there are two objectives for the policy, one long term and the other short term. It may be that the inevitable weight which has been placed on the short term because of short term financial pressures will make the long term policy more difficult to achieve. If so, this will be a great pity, because there is a long term moral case for a fairer and more logical distribution of incomes. A policy for a fairer distribution of incomes would stand a better chance if it was associated with a high wages policy and not a low wages policy. A high wages policy is logical in a country where labour is scarce and likely to be scarcer, whereas a low wages policy encourages its wasteful use. But without adequate financial reserves we cannot make the transition from a low wages policy to a high wages policy without enormous risk to real earnings and employment, risks which no responsible person, however dedicated to high wages, would willingly take.

The OEDC studies of institutional bargaining, from which the idea of an incomes policy stemmed, were aimed at correcting the cost-push spiral, the institutional minuet of wages negotiations rather than the demand pull of wages drift. A national wages bargain, a plan to bring order into top-level institutional bargaining does nothing to stop the informal shop floor negotiation of plus rates which comes from a high demand for labour and shows up in the statistics as wages-drift. The Swedes, with all their experience, have not yet conquered this. Yet in the short run it is demand-pull which sets the pace and which must be corrected if labour costs are to remain internationally competitive. The hope is that if prices are held down by the other side of the policy, management will be dissuaded from conceding too much at shop floor level. There are two sides to every wages bargain.

I have tried in the Bristol speech to convey something both of the problems and of the imperative need to solve them, especially of the need to solve them without deflation. An incomes policy associated with a low growth of money wages is possible. An incomes policy associated, in addition, with deflation 'to make it work' is more difficult.

In the trades union speech on productivity I have also tried to set out the dilemmas facing government. It may seem that the speech concedes too much, that it places too much of the blame for our difficulties on the financial situation and lays too little emphasis on industry's responsibility for improving productivity. However, it is my honest opinion that this is the true balance, that our difficulties do largely arise from our financial situation. This is also the opinion, I believe of most trades unionists. I do not believe that it is right to give a false balance however worthy the cause. What I have tried to show is that, admitting the case that it is our financial constraints which have boxed us in, we must nevertheless depend heavily on improved productivity to get us out. To blame the unions for something they do not believe, and with some justice, to be their fault leads only to acrimony, not to fruitful cooperation.

The final part of the trades union speech deals with the need to base wages claims more on productivity and less on comparability and the need also to reconcile productivity, prices and incomes. While our financial reserves are not enough to carry a high-wages policy until it pays off in higher productivity, non inflationary productivity bargaining within the policy could achieve the same objective. There are formidable difficulties. Productivity committees could be the institutional means, but the unions would have to concede to them some bargaining powers and management would have to concede to them some of the information now exclusively in management hands.

The response to the speech was encouraging but realistic. It was pointed out that unions worked in the dark and needed to know much more than they did if they were to base a claim on potential productivity improvements in such a way as to convince the other side. They also pointed to the practical difficulties in getting over the initial hurdle of

L   161

the need to change the pace and method of working while giving away most of the benefits of potential improvement. But my impression was that they thought it was well worth trying.

Government policies to break the inflationary spiral are not new. In the early 1960s we had Mr Selwyn Lloyd's wages freeze and in the mid-1950s we had Mr Macmillan's price plateau. Mr Maudling, when he was Chancellor, tried very hard to get agreement with the unions on wages policy. Indeed, we have had, ever since the war, warnings from one Government after the other on the dangers of pricing ourselves out of export markets. So present policy is not a new idea launched on the scene by a Labour Government, it is a continuation of an attempt that all Governments, Labour and Conservative, have made since the war to get the inflationary spiral under control. Nor is it in this Government, as is sometimes implied, just the responsibility of one Department or one Minister. It is, and has been, a collective Government responsibility to introduce it and it is a collective responsibility on the part of all the Government to implement it. The main differences between this policy and its predecessors are first of all that it deals with prices as well as incomes. This is aimed to give wage earners a tangible *quid pro quo* in stable prices. A second difference is that it deals not only with wages but with all forms of money income. Thirdly, there has been agreement, in a formal manner, not only on prices and incomes but also on the means of attaining higher earnings through productivity. Finally, there is now a National Board as the agreed full-time machinery to operate the policy. These are all very considerable strides forward compared with the attainments of previous Governments, Labour or Conservative.

Now you may well ask why have the Government spent so much time and effort in trying to achieve success in this policy of restraint which is politically a very thankless task. There are two reasons for this, one short term and one long term, and they are somewhat different in kind. At present the short term is the more vital to our success and prosperity as a nation. It is a hard fact, and there is no getting away from it, that at the beginning of 1964 our first line gold and dollar reserves were about £900M sterling and it is also a fact that the balance of payments deficit in 1964 was £750M and that as a direct result, when the bills had come in and the short-term fluctuations evened out, by January 1965, the reserves net of the new international loans raised by the Government were £150M, which is £750M less than the amount that they had been a year before. I am not telling you anything that has not been said before, I am just reminding you of it—in fact you can see it all set out on the front cover of this week's *Investors' Chronicle* in graphic form. Our short-term ability to meet our international obligations thus consists mainly of international loans given us on condition that we balance our current international payments in the fairly near future. Every Government has an implied obligation to look after the funds that are deposited with it, but we now have a more explicit obligation. There is no alternative to putting the balance of payments right. Our Government has given its word, and it must and will keep it. In the short run the only practical method of making sure that we get our trading accounts balanced is by making certain that our wages and prices are internationally competitive. Export drives, productivity bargaining, new industrial capacity, improved industrial efficiency, all have got to be brought to bear but you cannot be sure that they will bite in the time, by the end of next year. In the short term you can only rely on marginal improvement in price competitiveness over your international competitors. Other policies will pay off at some point but you do not know when. Indeed, some of them cannot in the nature of things, pay off for quite a long time ahead.

The long run aim of a policy on prices and incomes includes this objective of international competitiveness. If we do manage to conquer inflation and other countries do not, our internationally competitive position improves with every passing year, though of course, there are other ways than the holding down of money incomes to improve productivity in the long run, and in the long run a prices and incomes policy is only one factor in international competitiveness. But in the long run the policy also includes the objective of social justice. Is this going to be a country where the gains always go to those who are industrially best organised to make sure that they get their share? Does the wage earner really want his ability to participate fully in the growth of national wealth to depend on his ability to exploit a shortage for the time being of his skill or a temporary general shortage of labour? Can he depend on this going on for ever? Do we want, as a nation, bargaining power to slip out of the hands of the responsible union leader and into the 'catch as catch can' on the shop floor, where even the shop stewards cannot be certain of keeping control and delivering their end of the bargain?

If we want, in the long run, as a country, the nurses, the doctors, the teachers, the police, the soldiers, the sailors, the technicians which we should have, then those people too have got to keep their place, and if we want those who have no skill on which they can depend and who live outside the big southern conurbations to keep a decent standard, we have got to look after them too and see that there is the machinery to enable them to keep their place in the community and not to fall hopelessly behind. I am perfectly certain that it is because of these long-term aims that the union leaders have agreed to this policy and that they would not have agreed—as they have not agreed in the past—with a short-term policy of wages freeze simply to get out of our present difficulties.

You may say, that all this is fine and sensible, but we have got to face the facts of life, that there are strong reasons for companies to concede higher earnings when labour is scarce as it is at present, and strong temptations to pass on higher prices when everyone is working to capacity as they are at present. Does this policy, you may ask and I have no doubt you do ask, really face the facts of economic life? Well, of course, the policy at present agreed is a voluntary policy, there is no compulsion to obey the findings of the board.* It is, therefore, open to people to support the policy and it is open to them to try to destroy it. But it is the custom in this old democratic country

* Even under the proposed legislation, there is no obligation to follow the findings of the board. The legislation is mainly concerned to enable the board to find the facts and to ensure a standstill while it does so.

to try to work a voluntary policy if you possibly can. Most of our social order comes, not from legal obligations, but from voluntary restraint. It is most unusual in this country of ours for a policy, which most people in Britain agree is right, to fail simply because it is voluntary. If it does fail on this account then we really have taken a long step backwards. This is the difference, to my mind, between realism and cynicism. I sincerely hope that the time has not yet come in Britain where we have to look on every difficult proposal in an utterly cynical way. Let us be realistic, but do not let us try to be cynical. If we no longer have the self-restraint to take a short-term risk of minor loss for a long-term benefit of substantial gain, then something really has gone wrong with our character.

Personally, I do not just believe that our moral backbone has gone to that extent. This, after all, does give the wage earner something more than he had before. What has he got from the increase in money wages on average? Some have got more, but some have got less. On average I think real increases arising out of the increase in money wages less the cost of rising prices is no more than 2% a year. The norm is based on an assessment of what could be done in the future if we get our export and import balance right and that gives 3½% which is half as much again. Turning to the other side of the bargain, what does the businessman risk in hard cash by getting this policy off the ground, by absorbing the increase in wages over productivity for the first year? Perhaps he may put at risk, if all goes wrong, a sizeable chunk of the first year's profits, but this is very little in the balance if we really do get the growth of national income which a successful policy should give us. If you hold your prices, so will your competitors, they are bound to keep in line with you so that you will be no worse off than your competitor. This, will help to achieve price stability and the wages side of the policy begins to stand a chance.*

The transition is an extremely difficult point in the policy. There has undoubtedly been some jumping the gun on wages and prices and this makes it hard to draw a firm line at a given point on either wages or prices. Although it is the Government's

* On the whole this is how the policy did in fact work out in the first year.

job to give a lead, the Government has now done this and it therefore must, from now on, in a voluntary policy, depend on you to support it as, through your national leaders, you have agreed to do so. The FBI and the Chambers of Commerce and the other bodies have pledged themselves collectively to support it and as Sir Peter Runge pointed out yesterday, the pledge that has been made must be honoured. Success or failure is, therefore, largely in your hands. There are two sides to every wages bargain, those who receive and those who pay, and there are two sides to every invoiced price, those who charge and those who pay. You are in both bargains. You are not automatons. You have the 'make or break' decision for a voluntary policy.

The Government has got certain sanctions even in a voluntary policy. All is not sweet reason. It is not really in the interest of the officials of any union that an agreement that they have made at national level, should be seen to be made ridiculous. The union leaders, I have no doubt, want to make this policy successful and they have staked some of their reputation on the success of the policy. The authority of a union official lies in his ability to deliver his side of the bargain and the position of a union in the long run, too, depends on its ability to keep public support. If the public are told that a union claim is unjustified, then the position, although the policy is voluntary, is not exactly the same as it was before. On prices too, when the board pronounce against an increase the position is not the same as it was before. It would be more than a buyer's job is worth to be found by his boss paying the higher price that the board have said was unjustified. Nor can I imagine that the housewife will ignore the advice that the board gives her. I can only imagine that there will be a certain amount of anxiety on the part of most people to keep out of the limelight of public scrutiny that the board will give, that this will have an increasing effect on price decisions throughout industry and this in turn should have its effect on wages drift.

Now, if the voluntary method was to fail,* what are the

* The proposed legislation does not, as I have pointed out above, affect the voluntary principle in the carrying out of the board's recommendations.

alternatives that we are offered to this voluntary and, I think, British way of doing things? There may be some who feel that all will go on as before—a little bit of inflation, a little bit of stop-go, but a reasonable living for businessmen who do not want all the excitement of economic growth but just want to go on making a quiet and decent living. Or some may feel that a bit of financial wizardry will probably turn up and, after all this balance of payments business is a purely financial affair which should not affect our real resources. Well, that may have been true before 1964, but it is not true any more. The slump of 1929/31 was a purely financial affair, but it killed a lot of businesses stone dead and put unemployment into the millions and no Government is going to take chances with international financial confidence, especially a Government which is in charge of one of the world's two reserve currencies. Equally, no Government of a democracy, in an age when the technical and economic means of growth abound as never before, is going to tell the wage earner that he cannot have economic growth. So we have got to have financial probity on the one hand, and this I am sure we will have, and we have got to have economic growth on the other. These are two compulsions that will go on.

The other argument going the rounds is that we should really leave all of this to the purity of economic competition nationally and internationally. But the people who make this argument do not always spell out the consequences. In order to keep down prices internationally, the prescribed remedy is heavy deflation. Before the Government's regional policies have time to take effect, unemployment outside the southern conurbations has to be high enough to take some of the pressure of labour out of those conurbations. In the long run it is this Government's intention, as it was the last Government's intention, to try to correct regional imbalance. Meantime, how much unemployment do you need in Scotland to take the steam out of the demand for labour in Birmingham? Massive regional unemployment is at present the only way by which this particular policy of leaving it to the market economy alone could work.

Is that really the way to a better Britain? Leaving it to the

167

market economy means enforcing competition in prices not by a voluntary body before which you can appear, make your case, and make such adjustments yourself afterwards as seem to be correct, but by the massive legal superstructure of anti-trust, as operated by the Americans. I cannot imagine any businessman who has any experience of anti-trust legislation, would really choose that rather than to make a case to a body of living compatriots. If you are still doubtful, and think that maybe that is a better way, I refer you not only to the rate of unemployment in the United States but to a comparison of the rate of bankruptcies in Britain and in the United States. Even if, as some of the undiluted market economy school argue, what we really need is what they call a healthier rate of bankruptcy, deflation only makes our condition in Britain worse in the long run. What we need is confidence in sustained economic growth if we are to get rid of restrictive practices and to get the rate of investment in new capacity from which growth comes. Every single study that I have looked at since I have taken on this job seems to indicate what we need is not new capacity created by deflation of demand, but new capacity created by positive additional new investment, that is the way out in the long run. Every deflation makes labour guard its work more closely and makes the businessman mark down the size of the market for which he invests. This is no way forward for Britain. We must have confidence in the economy and this cannot come by recurrent bouts of deflation which only make the next turn in the cycle worse.

Now, at the other extreme, which is not talked of so much nowadays, there are those who would rely on the massive imposition of controls. I need hardly argue to you as business-men on the way in which price controls could throw sand into the delicate mechanism of pricing. Nor need I point out the problems of policing which would be needed to make sure that there was no reduction in quality or specification at the frozen price or on the problem of the man who has to pay a higher price for his imports, but whose own prices are pegged. These examples have only to be given to show the difficulties of a control of prices. This has not stopped governments of some countries from using a device like this from time to time. I am sure, however, that you would all want to go a very long way to make sure that this never seemed to be the only way out for a British Government. But if you are looking for an alternative to a prices and incomes policy, this is an alternative and it does have its advocates.

I have left one alternative until last because it is the one which appeals most to all those engaged in industry, both management and unions, and certainly it was the one that appealed most to me as manager. This is to promote policies which will make sure that productivity rises fast enough to absorb even the current rate of increase in money earnings. I could see, as most managers and trades unionists can, tremendous scope for increasing productivity in the companies and industries for which we work. American wage rates are over twice British wage rates, so you can argue that our problem is not really one of the internationally high level of our wages. The Europeans have been fast catching up with our wage rates and even the Japanese are beginning to pay Western rates of wages. The pressure for greater productivity, so one argues, must come from higher wages as well as competitive prices. How otherwise can you force management to introduce labour-saving equipment if it continues to be more economic to use cheap labour instead of machines? The American standard of living is high because Americans had found ways of paying high wages and still keeping costs down. They have done it because high wages forced them to do it. What, after all, are we aiming for but a higher real standard of living? Provided prices are competitive—and personally I have never been in an industry where they were not—why should rising wages not provide the pressure for increased efficiency? I remember arguing all this vigorously with one of the members of the old National Incomes Commission. Looked at from a company level this seems a very reasonable policy but looked at from a national level I have now discovered it seems still desirable but not nearly so practicable.

In the first place, it does not meet the short-term situation. Higher American wages, when you go into it, come in part from higher physical investment and investment takes time to put down and will be much more forthcoming when the balance of payments problem is on the way to solution. It will not answer for the next two to three years. Then what the manager in the keenly competitive industry does not see is the situation in the less competitive sectors of the economy, where a wage increase of 5% gets passed on as a price increase of 5% and that means a profit increase of at least 5% and often much more. To get competitive conditions may in turn need more investment and some surplus capacity and this again takes time, because it is when you are running right up to capacity that competition is at its weakest.

In the second place, those of us who are in productive industry are only part of the working population and a policy of allowing industrial wages to take all of the improvement in productivity leads to a mounting differential between production wages and the wages of all those who are in services, however essential, like doctors, and teachers. Something has got to be left over for them in the shape of lower prices, and it must not just be a left-over, it has got to be enough in the long run to attract the right people into these services. It must fulfil the criterion, too, of long-term social justice.

Thirdly, and this is a factor that really did not impress itself on me until I went into Government service, there are certain overriding limitations on the rate of economic growth for the economy as a whole. An industry, or a company, in which you happen to be taking part may be able to grow at the rate of 10% and still get the electric power, the water, the roads, the vehicles, the raw materials and all the other things it needs from outside. But you cannot switch the whole economy to a 10% growth rate in a year in order to pay, for instance, for an 8% increase in earnings. The public sector expenditure, particularly on power, does have to be a bit ahead of the growth in industrial capacity to take up the peaks, but it cannot be put too far ahead without taking the resources that would slow down everything else. It takes time to put down power stations and all the rest of the industrial infrastructure which is needed to sustain economic expansion.

Finally, there is the whole question of the redeployment of people involved in a very rapid switch to a much higher growth rate. This also takes time. There is a rate at which you can switch jobs and homes and skills and patterns of life and maintain an ordered growth that may be more than 4% a year, but there is an overall rate beyond which this cannot be done without suffering and confusion. Any attempt to do so would be worse than self-defeating and we would not get our growth rate in the end.

Although the way out is through higher productivity in the long run, this is not the whole answer in the short run — we cannot move the whole economy that fast. There is an overriding limit to the improvement in the rate of growth that we can make in the economy in the short run, but, of course, in the long run, higher living standards can only come from higher productivity, and all the arguments linking growth with productivity are right in a five to ten year period. There is therefore no reason why, in the late 1960s, the norm for real increases in earnings should not be higher than it is is now and in the 1970s it could be still higher with continuing price stability. Tough and difficult though this policy is, and tough and difficult though the financial situation is, nevertheless we have the reserves of skill, the reserves of energy and the self discipline to see us through this tough patch and out to the road ahead. In the meantime, it does seem to me that this prices and incomes policy is necessary for our short-term economic welfare as well as for long-term social justice and that in one way or another it will have to be carried out.

.   .   .

I think I am speaking for all of us when I say that to anyone with any knowledge of industry, improvement in industrial output seems to be not only necessary and desirable but a very part of our way of life. We are so close to technical change, we know how far it has taken us and can take us, what enormous potential is as yet untapped, that it is almost incredible that anyone could be content with a situation where annual output increased by only 1 or 2%. If we are required to tighten our belts when other countries can grow by anything between 5

and 10% a year, when American income per head is 150%
higher than ours, then something must be wrong somewhere.
You would think that this was obvious to everyone, but it isn't.
We still have elderly gentlemen writing from addresses in the
deepest countryside to tell us that the country is going to rack
and ruin, that we have lost our moral fibre, that we need
politicians with the guts to tell the country the truth and as
often as not—as well you know—implying that it is the fault
of those selfish trade unionists. Most of them sound as if they
have never seen a shop steward or union official in their lives.

Further, even those with some knowledge of industry and
who have influence on industrial policies seem to be curiously
unaware of the potential economic growth which new technology now makes possible. There are economists with quite a
respectable following in academic circles who are oddly
pessimistic on economic growth and the industrial facts of life. I
think that possibly their disbelief in economic growth arises
because they base themselves on historic data and predict
the future almost entirely by extrapolation of the past. This
means that an assumption is made that any constraints on
economic growth which have affected the past will inevitably
affect the future. Sometimes these constraints are known,
sometimes they can only be guessed at and sometimes they are
unknown. If they are unknown, there is no way of getting them
out of the projections. But whether known or unknown they
are built into the predictions and tend, therefore, to be self-
perpetuating. 'Because it has only been $2\frac{1}{2}$% in the past and
we have no evidence that it will be higher in future, we predict
$2\frac{1}{2}$% for the future.' So the low figure gets written into the
market forecasts and business expansion is based on this slow
growth. It does not matter that American output per head is
over twice our output per head, that technology is racing ahead,
a fractional percentage increase above the historic trend-line
is treated as being wildly optimistic.

There is also a curiously cautious attitude towards economic
growth among a lot of people in commerce—whether they
trade in commodities, money, shares or insurance risks—
even though their interests are strongly linked to buoyant

industrial growth. The reasons for their cautious attitude towards economic growth are harder to fathom, but it is basically, I believe, because although industrial expansion is profitable, the short-term interests of the commerce and industry tend to look different. Commerce, of course, does not depend entirely on British industry. It cares, among other things, for Britain's enormous overseas investments. We have, according to the latest Bank of England Review, assets overseas of £15,000M of which £10,000M is in industry. This money is not invested in British industry, it is invested in foreign industry and its profitability depends on the growth not of the British economy but of foreign economies. But this in itself, of course, creates a self-perpetuating constraint in the British economy. The more other economies prosper relative to the British economy, the greater the tendency for funds to flow abroad. But the greater the capital flow from Britain, the worse the balance of payments and the slower the British economy can grow. The more people invest abroad the more it seems to pay them to do so. So we tend to get a long-term drain on capital account.

Commerce, of course, wants a free flow of funds and no control on capital movements or if there is they want it to be of short duration. They argue that no one has ever gone short of capital at home because of capital outflow. But this is not the point. If the capital outflow is a constraint on the balance of payments, it reduces the rate of growth and with it the demand for capital. It is somewhat irrelevant to complain that I have no appetite if you have a firm grip on my windpipe. The fact is that the capital outflow is by far the biggest single drain on the balance of payments and makes relatively little contribution to British industry's ability to compete in world markets. As a result of this steady capital drain we now have these enormous sums invested in foreign industry while our own economic growth has been held down.

There are a number of arguments in favour of this investment in foreign economies and it is only fair to put them. First of all, it is argued that we have for most of this century depended on our 'invisible income' from these investments to

meet our deficit on visible trade. This is true, but it begs the
question, which is why do we have the gap on visible trade?
What brings in more currency, investment in British industry
or investment in a foreign industry? It is a fact that British
manufacturing industry exports 35% of its output and this
ratio has been fairly constant. It is arguable that new investment produces a higher proportion of exports. If you take
reasonable capital output ratio on new investment as being $3\frac{1}{2}$: 1
then investment in UK manufacturing industry should bring
in currency revenue of 10%.* But it is thought that investment
in overseas companies has brought in currency revenue of
not much more than 4%.† Further, even if this was a pessimistic assumption, the fact is that we pay half as much again
in foreign currency for the short-term borrowing needed to
finance the investment overseas as we seem to receive as a
currency return on our capital invested.

Secondly, it is argued that we have to invest abroad in order
to promote our own exports and some large companies have
some very convincing balance of payments for their own companies to prove this. The argument goes that developing
countries will increasingly put down their own industries and
if we are to keep the markets we built up, we must put our
own assembly plants down in order to retain the exports of
components. I have some sympathy with this because my own
old company was knocked out of market after market because
of tariffs and quotas raised against us in favour of local infant
industries. But I think we were just unlucky. Two-thirds of
Britain's exports go to Europe and North America where the
rules of GATT apply with full force and where the whole
effort of the signatories is to reduce tariffs and barriers to trade
through the Kennedy Round and other tariff negotiations.
While it is true that the underdeveloped countries will make
some manufacturing investment, their rate of capital formation

---

* From this has to be deducted the currency costs of extra imports of raw materials, but in technically advanced industries these should be low.

† Studies are currently in hand on this figure. To arrive at it one must of course
deduct foreign tax. The balance can be calculated as a percentage of dividends
remitted to initial investment or a percentage of after-tax profit to current worth.

is small and they can only manufacture on a very limited range of goods. If, however, they do invest in a particular industry they are likely, in the end, to go the whole hog and to leave no room for imported components. I have had the experience of exporting less and less to an overseas subsidiary as the local industry grew, until finally nil quotas were placed on all our exports from this country. We were fortunate to find a buyer for the company. At best, therefore, this is an interim and not a long-term solution of our balance of payments. It is interesting to note that our trading competitors with the highest growth of exports have had minimal overseas investment, but a much higher investment in their own industries. However, even if there is a marginal case on export grounds for investment in foreign companies which we control, there is none for investment in foreign companies which we do not control. But 40% of our industrial investment overseas is 'portfolio' investment, which is in quoted securities which are, for the most part, not controlled by the UK investor.

Thirdly, it is argued, in favour of overseas investment including portfolio investment, that it has increased enormously in value over the years and that this gives substantial backing to our reserves. But it is only fair to ask whether British investment would not have increased as much in value if we had allowed ourselves the same rate of economic growth as the foreigner, had we not had the constraint on our balance of payments caused by investing in foreign industry. Nor is private overseas investment, in fact, much use to our reserves. To be of use, it would have to be in the hands of Government; it would then have to be sold on foreign stock exchanges for cash without unduly depressing the market and the cash would have to be transferred across the exchange without causing undue financial strain on the country which was losing the currency. No doubt these assets have been of some help in raising loans and there is a large block already in Government hands. No doubt also they can and will be liquefied gradually under the present arrangements for transferring a quarter of all sales of portfolio investment to the reserves. But this is not much of an argument for investing overseas what could be invested in the

UK without any cost to the exchanges, especially if the UK investment brings in greater currency revenue.

My own view is that the true interests of British commerce must be overwhelmingly in favour of having a strong British industry. Most of British capital is in British industry.* Most of the business done by British commerce arises in this country. We cannot have a strong commercial community on a weak industrial base. But if we have a strong industrial base, we will have a strong and prosperous commercial community.

The second largest drain on our balance of payments is defence. Three days after the publication of the Defence White Paper it is not necessary to go into much detail on this subject. It also looks like being a rather hotter political subject than a civil servant—even though temporary—ought to tackle. But it is at least clear from the White Paper that the Government are making strenuous efforts to cut defence costs, especially the overseas costs of defence. The period in which our overseas costs of defence went up as our overseas possessions declined seems to have come to an end. Some people think that this could be tailed off faster, some may think it is too fast. That is the area of political difference. But I will be very surprised if, in five to ten years' time, we have not cut our own overseas costs of defence to a point which is much fairer in relation to our comparative interests around the globe. I find it hard to believe that if we started with a clean sheet we would be spending our money in quite the way we do. We cannot have a clean sheet in one or two years, but in five to ten years there is little we cannot change if we set our minds to it.

The third largest drain is aid.† This costs about £200M and it is estimated very roughly that exports compensate for possibly as much as £100M of this—though I would regard this

* The average institutional investor has, and must continue to have, an over-whelmingly higher stake in the success of his British portfolio than he has in the success of his foreign portfolio.

† Only the USA has a higher proportion of Gross Domestic Product going to defence and aid. But more of our defence has to be paid for in foreign currency than America's and though France comes close behind us in aid, the currency cost of French aid is thought to be low.

as a high estimate. Most people agree that help to developing countries has a high priority but it is easy to forget that what really helps these countries is a rapidly growing demand for their products. This brings in far more revenue than aid can ever do. Economic stagnation here is ruination for them. We need, therefore, to pitch our aid level where it does not stop our economic growth.

These three major burdens are the real cause of our slow economic growth as compared with other countries, but there is one notable exception. That exception is the United States of America. But they have two and a half times our wage rates and over twice our productivity. They have demonstrated the tremendous gains which are available in productivity through better management and higher investment. So that although we are, to some extent, boxed in financially the US example shows that there is a way out through higher productivity.

We are not of course entirely boxed in financially. The Government have done a great deal to stop the outflow of capital. Defence costs have been cut. Aid has been held level. A temporary surcharge has been put on imports. Exports have gone up by 7% and imports only fractionally and the trading account—visible and invisible—has gone from the marginal surplus of 1964 to a normal surplus in 1965. But, in the meantime, because the financial constraints on the economy take time to move we need all the help we can get from productivity. So having examined the way in which we have got into our troubles, we now come to the way out, which I believe to lie in a big improvement in productivity.

A lot of people still talk of productivity as if it were a matter of urging people to dig harder or turn a handle faster, as if the whole problem were a matter of willingness to work. Of course, there are places where this is true. But, by and large, I believe that improved productivity is a matter of more industrial engineering and more hardware. This is, in turn, a matter mainly for management. But how do we encourage management to improve the productivity of the companies they direct and manage? And who is going to encourage them? Who will they listen to? First of all, managers will listen to other managers, especially those in their own industry. One of the objects of the Economic Development Committees is to point out the action which needs to be taken in a particular industry if it is to improve its economic performance. When the little Neddy comes out with an action programme it is signed and endorsed by the half dozen top management representatives of the industry. The industry may not always quite agree with it but they are bound to respect it and our experience is that, quietly and without fuss or publicity, the balls gets rolling.

Secondly, managers will listen to their shareholders. The new Companies Bill looks a bit dry but it is my guess that it is going to be one of the most effective measures of this Government. I am glad to see that it has the general support of all parties in Parliament. It is going to put the searchlight on some dusty corners and I shall be very surprised if some businesses which have not had, until now, to publish their accounts either because they were private or because they were hiding in the corner of some giant *mixum gatherum* industrial empire, do not suddenly shake themselves up and start working if only for the reputation of those who run them. I have come across several cases lately where one or two divisions of a group of companies had been carrying the rest on their shoulders for years.

Thirdly, managers will listen to those who work for them and here we come to the punch-line of this talk. I have never in all my experience as a manager had a trades unionist come to me to tell me that we could pay higher wages if we were more efficient. Every claim I have ever looked at has been based on the cost of living or comparability. Yet who is in a better position to talk about the efficiency of a company than the unions? It has members in every company in the industry. It has an almost instantaneous grapevine for comparing the situation from plant to plant on hours, conditions, basic rates, overtime rates, manning scales on particular types of plant — and everything else that affects the work of individuals in industry. Union leaders can tell you with precision which companies are well-managed and which are not. I have had union leaders in my office outlining the needs of particular industries right down to the kind of plant which is needed and the places where it has already been installed abroad. Who else can compare company with company and plant with plant? The knowledge is there, and the opportunity is there but, so far, very few unions in this country have made use of it.

I realise that there are difficulties. I can only guess at what they are. I imagine that arguments on comparability and cost of living are easier to establish and are hallowed by precedent. They are in the long tradition of fairness and equity without which unions would hardly exist. I imagine also that there are not enough people in full-time employment by the union to do the groundwork necessary to launch that type of claim and sustain it in the face of the numbers who would be put to argue from the other side. I realise too that greater efficiency can not only mean more tons turned out per man, it can also mean fewer men per ton. Finally, I realise that even Government, with all its anxiety about productivity, is still more immediately worried about inflation and is naturally worried that so-called 'non-inflationary' wage awards would turn out to be inflationary after all. Before going on, it may be as well to pause on this point and explain the dilemma.

It is a fact that a limited number of companies have the experience to conduct non-inflationary wage awards geared to productivity. These give a proportion of the increase in productivity in wage awards or productivity bonuses and the company retains the balance to improve its competitive position, to pay out in higher dividend or to plough back into the business. However, in conditions of full employment this increase in the wages paid by some companies puts pressure on the other companies in the area to pay the same to keep the labour or to try their own hand at non-inflationary wage awards tied to productivity. It is all too easy to turn a non-inflationary award into an inflationary award by a bit of simple mishandling. What most people forget is that enough has to be left over from extra pay to direct production workers (where the increase is easily measured) to give extra pay to maintenance engineers and others, not on the production line, whose work is more difficult to measure. Supervisory grades will also need a share otherwise they begin to see their differentials rapidly disappearing.

What the Government also has to remember is that the principles of comparability will very properly be invoked when industrial wages, which can be measured directly against their contribution to productivity, go ahead faster than wage awards to teachers, nurses, the armed forces, the police and others who cannot engage in productivity bargaining. So a simple productivity bonus to direct production workers cannot be allowed to take all the increase in productivity. In the perfect world, of course, a high wage economy would force business to look at ways of off-setting higher costs in reduced prices and awards based on productivity would not be inflationary either directly or indirectly. But the constraints on the British balance of payments do not allow us to experiment with a high-wage economy and all our experience until this year is that wage awards do get passed on, for the most part, in higher prices, leaving only a residual of about 2% increase in real standard of living from higher productivity.

My own guess is that although pressure on the labour market is our immediate cause of inflation, a slow expectation of growth is a more fundamental cause. When a businessman finds himself in a market with a relatively slow rate of growth and operating at full capacity, he may well feel that he gains more than he risks by increasing prices. On the other hand, in a rapidly expanding market, where a great deal of new capacity is being put down to meet the expansion, he will probably feel that he risks a good deal more in the long run than he gains in the long run by increasing prices. In the latter case, it is vital to him to keep his share of an expanding market. There is a prize ahead worth fighting for. If others are investing for the same prize and there is spare capacity in the industry, it will not pay him, even in the short run, to risk his volume by raising his price. The more highly capitalised the industry, the more will this be true.

The conditions for a really non-inflationary industry are a buoyant long-term growth of demand together with a slightly more buoyant increase in industrial investment. These are also the conditions for a better import/export balance. It is notable that in the period of British industrial dominance in the nineteenth century there was a steady long-term lowering of prices. This was based on a series of major technical breakthroughs. The breakthroughs to our hand for the second industrial revolution are as great in magnitude as for the first if only we care to try our hands upon them.

What then can be done by unions within the present constraints to see that we get the higher productivity which will help to remove the constraints for good and all?

First, I would urge you to use the Economic Development Committees to the full. They cover the bulk of industry and distribution. Each covers on average 400,000 people in employment, so they are worth while in terms of time and effort but near enough to the practical decisions to be able to make useful and down-to-earth proposals. However desirous the Government and other members may be to see the management of the industry take action to obtain higher productivity, the union representatives are in a quite unique position to judge the improvement in productivity available and the means needed to bring it about. Here is a tremendous opportunity which is open to you to pick up.

Second, I think we need to work out an agreed code of practice on productivity bargaining so that a non-inflationary wage award really is non-inflationary and so that the idea of productivity bargaining can have the wholehearted support of those who hesitate now because of the very real inflationary risks. We must have agreement on the costs to be set off against the improvement in productivity, including the cost of new capital equipment and the cost of all the consequential increases in pay which will have to be given on grounds of comparability to those in a plant or company whose work is not directly measurable and who cannot, therefore, have an increase based directly on productivity. We must also have some recognition of the effect of the total of productivity awards on those not in manufacturing industry. This can best be done by writing into a formula some allowance for price reduction.

Indeed a three-way split of the improvement between management, unions and customers of genuine improvements in productivity would seem to be both watertight against inflation and to be enough to make it worth while for both parties to have a go. It is usually better to have a bit of cake than no cake at all.

Lastly, I think we will in the end need some sort of forum at company or plant level where both sides can keep the opportunities from higher productivity continually under review. This is the toughest job of all because it laps over into the provinces both of the straightforward wage negotiation machinery and of management decisions. Nevertheless, the Government are, as you know, studying the idea and hope, in due course, to come out with some proposals for discussion.*

---

* Although the difficulties of applying this idea on a wide scale are formidable, nevertheless there are companies which have applied it with great success and I am sure therefore that it is well worth the time and effort which will be needed to secure its adoption on a wider scale.

CHAPTER TWELVE

Regional Policy —Investing in a Balanced Community

This talk was given to the Ulster Societies at Birmingham in October 1965. I have included it because I believe that economic development must take into account physical and social environment if it is not to destroy our small islands and our whole social fabric.

The Ulster Societies are local societies of Ulstermen living in the rest of the United Kngdom. It was rather appropriate that the meeting should have been in Birmingham which is one of the centres attracting new population and expatriate Ulstermen. There were, unfortunately, no questions, so I had no reaction from the talk. It was splashed in the Belfast Telegraph, *reported correctly in a dozen lines in* The Times *and the bit on Kensington bed-sitters was picked up by* The Daily Telegraph.

Although I have hesitated in the talk to come out wholeheartedly in favour of regional government, my personal inclination is increasingly in that direction. If we join the European Economic Community it will be even more important to stop the drift to the more powerful economic centres, and this can, I believe, only be done by strengthening the power of each region. Since the talk was given there has been the announcement of the Commission on Local Government, so that the questions of the form, strength and boundaries of government outside Westminster will now be examined again. My hope is that the Commission will propose not just the improvement of local government by marginally bigger units, but will see the need for provincial government which is big enough to tackle the substantial jobs which are best done outside Whitehall. I hope too that it will have the political accountability necessary to shift regional decisions from the overloaded machine of Whitehall and West-minster and allow national Government to get on with the problems which can and must be solved on national level. It would be a real tragedy if the regional councils have been set up only to find themselves,

*in the end, outside the main stream of provincial and local government.
I am sure that they are a basis on which we can build.*

Fewer and fewer people today belong by birth to the place
where they live. I was born where the river Moyola flows into
Lough Neagh. My father had been born there and his father
and so on for two centuries or more. None of us lives there now.
I now have a house in one of the older suburbs of London.
We are a neighbourly family and know the people on both
sides of us and several other families in the road, which has
about 100 houses. As for the rest, they are and will probably
remain complete strangers. The children can never go into
the street where the traffic thunders down day and night. They
only know the children they go to school with. Very few people
enjoy the communal life of a church any more. There is no
other community centre, no sense of belonging to any group
of people who care what you do or why you do it. Occasionally
from one of the nearby bed-sitters one has a glimpse of terrible
loneliness and misery—husbands who have left their wives,
wives who have divorced their husbands, living in single rooms
alone with their thoughts. Yet this community is, in a way, a
better one than most. It is old enough to have some roots.
It is not socially stratified; it has a mixture of rich and poor,
young and old. It has not been swallowed up in a rapid sprawl
of identical housing units as have some smaller, less distinct
communities.

But this is a far cry from the sort of community into which
most of us were born. My grandfather knew his neighbours
and was known by them for miles around. When the Moyola
overflowed in 1926 neighbours with high barns and houses
helped those without. People knew my grandfather's political
affiliations, and his religious convictions. They knew his family
history. If my father or his brothers or sisters got up to any
mischief, the whole neighbourhood knew. And my grandfather
and his family knew as much about the neighbours and their
children. When it came to intermarriage, they knew what their
children were doing. They might not always agree with it, but
at least they knew. Now I am not saying that this was an idyllic

society. We know perfectly well that it was not. There was religious bitterness, there was fighting. There was suspicion and there was some oppressiveness in a close community where almost all your sins would find you out. No one would want to go back to the dark nights on isolated farms. But when I return to Ulster now that the worst of those days is behind, I still get the sense of a well-balanced community and a sense of belonging, of being more than a statistical digit, more than a stranger among strangers and I have a sense of the continuity of traditions which are more than habits and idiosyncracies. I believe that human beings need this sense of community and that society will perish if it does not have it. But, at present, every economic and social pressure is driving us blindly in the other direction and, I believe, to the disintegration of society as we have known it. Let us have a look at these pressures.

First and foremost there is the pressure of higher industrial wages in the great industrial conurbations, especially in the South-East and the Midlands. Who is going to ask his wife to live on a small-holding in the Sperrins yielding £6 a week; who is going to be a draper's assistant in Magherafelt when he can earn £20 a week in a semi-skilled job across the water? And so there is the steady drain to the great motor plants and all the lesser plants which serve them and the other industries like them. When you have invested £25M in expensive machinery you do not mind paying a bit over the odds for labour to make the machinery work. You might wonder why, if labour is so short, the economic pressure does not bring the companies to the people instead of the other way round. Indeed, some of the companies do come, and no one has been more successful than the Northern Ireland Government in persuading them to do so. But for this Northern Ireland would be a depressed region. But only those who have tried to persuade business to move out of the English conurbations can know the strength of the forces which tend to keep it there. I remember talking to the managing director of a company making dictating machines. He told me that he had a couple of dozen men skilled in the key job of tuning and he would be lost without them. He knew they would not go out of London. He wanted, however, to put down a new factory outside London for some of the other work, but the works manager liked coarse fishing at Sunbury-on-Thames. So on every expedition to a prospective site they also had a look at the coarse fishing prospects; at each it was finally concluded that the fishing at Sunbury was better and so the factory had to stay in London.

Then there is the problem of industrial inter-dependence. In an area like Birmingham there is a great deal of sub-contracting. The subcontractor can aggregate long runs and he can specialise and can get his costs down below those of his customers. They come to depend on his shop as if it were one of their own and they probably have similar relations with 20 or 30 other specialists like him. They become so intertwined that they carry no stock and call off what they need from hour to hour. If anything is missing they can send down the road and have it at once. It takes a lot of courage to break this sort of dependence. It requires basic changes in organisation and much better control of stocks and better forecasting of requirements than is necessary with old-established subcontractors.

Thirdly, there is the problem of training in basic skills. A coalminer can become a metal worker in a remarkably short time, but the scrappage can be very high until he realises that you do not chuck metal around as you chuck coal around. Finally, there is the whole problem of inertia. Better the devil you know, say the management. We may have a labour turn-over of 30% and a difficult lot of shop stewards, we may have to come to a full-stop when a minor subcontractor has a strike, but Birmingham knows how to work in metal and who knows what problems we would meet elsewhere.

But the pull to the big cities is not just economic. Since time began men have been crowding into cities. They were only prevented by the appalling sanitation and recurrent bouts of the plague. But now we have sanitation more or less under control and in Western cities the plague is a thing of the past. A friend of mine, who enjoys climbing in the Andes, visited a remote Indian tribe in Peru just after the war. Most of them had never been over the mountain pass which he had just traversed. A few years later he went there again and found that the Peruvian Government had built a road over the pass. The only Indians left were the old folk. All the younger ones had got on the first lorry for the coast. They had no jobs and lived in appalling shanty towns, but the compulsion was apparently overwhelming.

People tend to rationalise the urge to go to the capital city by attributing it to better amenities. But the so-called amenities of civilisation are everywhere in Britain today, not just in big cities. The specialities of the capital city which really cannot be found in Belfast and Newcastle are very few indeed. In any case, they are much more frequented by visitors than by Londoners. The weather is said to be better, but anyone tramping the hot asphalt of London in July or August might well long for the breezes of Bangor and there is a peculiar penetration in the damp of a London winter fog which is rare elsewhere. The problem of travelling to work in London is notorious. There is little doubt that life outside the big conurbations is a great deal more civilised. Yet the imbalance between the South-East and the rest of the country continues to grow.

What is behind this urge to go to the great centres of population? It is not entirely economic, nor is it entirely social in the narrow sense of being in 'Society'. It is, I think, much more a sense of wanting to be at the centre of power, of wanting to be where the really big decisions are made. It is the pull of the metropolis against the provinces. It is the feeling that what goes on around you is no more than parish-pump politics, all about rates and drains, and that all the great issues of the day, the stuff of politics is being decided elsewhere. The European movement will not be decided, they feel, in Harrogate or Alderley Edge or the East of Suez issue in Port Talbot or Weston-super-Mare. And economic power follows political power. The great head offices are in London, Vickers Tower and the Shell Centre on both sides of Parliament. The great union headquarters, Transport and General, AEU and ETU, are all in London.

You may think I exaggerate the political pull of the capital. After all, not everyone is a budding politician, tycoon or union leader. In any case, everyone is represented at Westminster and in the democracy of trade unionism you do not have to live in London to have a vote. Business can have its head offices elsewhere, wool in Bradford, cotton in Manchester, Harland and Wolff in Belfast, Parsons and Reyrolle on Tyneside, Rolls-Royce in Derby, not to mention the great engineering companies, in Birmingham. That is true but it is equally true that these are, today, the exceptions. Many a company with provincial works has a London head office and the world of commerce, banking and insurance is increasingly concentrated in London. Nor must we minimise the attraction which power has, even for those who will never exercise it. Our means of communication are dominated in both press and television by national media. Few newspapers in the world can boast of a circulation of 5 million and a readership of 20 million. The American press is far more provincial, so is its television. The coast to coast hook-up is the exception not the rule. The news in this country, therefore, is dominated by national events and, as it comes over, that seems to be what matters. Even on local matters, the new motorway or by-pass, the new docks or airfield, the new plant, the men laid off because of short-time, the key decision seems so often to be taken in London and local leaders are photographed going into and out of the London offices where these decisions are made. Too often they seem to be protesting after the real decision has been taken, visibly powerless to halt the tide of events controlled by forces which appear to be beyond them. Of course the MP has the right to ask questions in the House and there is no doubt that local interests are taken into account. But the power to react is not in the same class as the power to initiate.

Before 1918 a great empire dominated South-East Europe. Its capitals were Vienna and Budapest, the capital of the twin-kingdom of Hungary. After the war, both were capitals, but of tiny states instead of an empire. The reason why we find so many Hungarians and Austrians today in prominent positions in Germany, Britain and America is not primarily because the economic position of these latter countries between the wars was better—in all three it was terrible—but because for the Hungarians and Austrians, power had moved elsewhere. What happened in Budapest and Vienna, which in the days of Metternich and Franz Joseph had made Europe tremble, was little more now than a sideshow. This, I think, illustrates two points—that transfers of power affect people but that the isoated city state is not an alternative—a sentiment with which every unionist will agree.

What then is the ideal balance of the community in which we want to live? Somewhere between the tiny isolated city-state which controls its own destinies completely, but matters to no one, and the monolithic state where all power resides at the centre, is there some mean at which we should aim? The mean which many countries today adopt is the Federal system. This is the system in the United States, Canada, Australia, India and, to a limited extent, Western Germany. It is interesting that none of those countries has a drift of population to the Federal capital. The Provincial capitals like Toronto, Montreal, Vancouver all have a greater pull than Ottowa. New York and San Francisco can compete with Washington; the Federal capitals of Melbourne and Sydney with Canberra; the land capitals like Munich and Dusseldorf with the Federal capital of Bonn. It is not just that here is a split between the political centre and the economic centre. Each one of the economic centres is also a centre of provincial power. Look at what happens when the movement is the other way. There was a time when Dublin was one of the great British cities. That was in the eighteenth century when an Irish Parliament sat in Dublin. No matter that no Parliament in those days was properly representative, Dublin was a centre of political power. As soon as this power was taken away it went into decline as a city. Dublin's heyday was in the eighteenth century as its architecture even today testifies.

You may say that a Federal system is all right in a country with a great population, such as America or in a country covering great areas such as Canada or Australia, but not for a small country such as the United Kingdom. Federal solutions to government are also of course more important where there are lasting ethnic or geographical differences between the parts of a nation. But if a new Federal system creates or

perpetuates differences — and to some extent building govern-
mental institutions on the differences does harden them — then it
is a force in the wrong direction. The Union at Westminster has
made one race of English, Welsh, Scots and Ulstermen (I used
to say Ulster Scots until I discovered that quite a lot of Ulstermen came from England). Give full Federal Parliaments back
and it might only perpetuate pedantic differentiation. A number
of my wife's elderly relations pointed out, when we announced
our engagement, that she would be the first member of the
family to marry outside Wales and I am grateful that no narrow
nationalism made these observations of more than passing
academic interest in the family! For this reason, if for no other, a
full-blooded Federal system for the United Kingdom as a
whole may be wrong.

In addition, our position in the world makes it necessary
that our central Government be strong. We have over 50 million
people on a small island without natural resources and maintain a knife-edge balance on trade and commerce, the second of
the world's two great reserve currencies and formidable
international defence commitments. We need a powerful and
responsive central Government and it is hard to have this
together with full Federal autonomy.

However, the argument that we are too small for any de-
centralisation of administrative power does not really stand up.
In population we are almost a third of the size of the United
States, which now has 50 states. On this basis alone, our
population is equivalent to over 16 American states. Canada's
population and Australia's are both less than a third of ours
and one has 9 Federal states and the other 7. The young Queen
Elizabeth II reigns over $2\frac{1}{2}$ times as many British subjects as
the young Queen Victoria and about 10 times as many as the
first Queen Elizabeth. Her Ministers administer a Government
machine which is certainly many times more complex. West
Germany, which has the same population allows considerable
autonomy to its Land governments. Finally, a country with as
long a history of successful democratic government as ourselves,
Switzerland has a population of only 5M, but considerable
cantonal authority and no visible drift to any of its cantonal

capitals. Geneva, Berne, Zurich, Lausanne are all important Swiss centres and none overwhelm the others.

As there are problems in the unit of power being too big, there are problems in its being too small. There is little doubt that local authorities find increasingly that they are unable to do full justice to the problems which face them because they are limited to the city or borough boundaries and the problems do not end at the city limits. A friend of mine is a doctor in a small town in Dorset. A few years ago he was fuming about the town drains. Next thing he knew he was on the council and within no time he was chairman. He is as public-spirited as the next man, but he assures me that he would never do it again. His overwhelming experience was of the impossibility of facing the problems of the modern world with the machinery of Government which can be provided on the rates of the urban district council. He is equally clear on the political impossibility of *ad hoc* amalgamation, having tried, in the interests of economy, to persuade the 'urban' to go in with the 'rural'. You may remember the story which was told in Belfast on the Queen's last official visit. The chairmen of the district councils were being presented in the Town Hall. The official read out the next in the line as 'Councillor McWatters of Ballyjamesmartin'. 'Indeed your Majesty, I am nothing of the kind, he has it all wrong. I am Councillor McWatters of Ballyjamesduff.'*

The way ahead may lie through the direct reform of local government but although I am not an expert in the subject I doubt it. It would take a long time and some of our problems will not wait. The physical crisis of the great conurbations is already upon us and the decisions made now will affect us for years ahead. This is a subject by itself, but anyone who knows the problems in physical planning, knows that the big decisions cannot be made within the city boundaries. Already we have consortia of local authorities for building schools and houses, but we have hardly begun to tackle the problem of urban

* Just in case there are any Councillors by the name of McWatters I would like to say that I made up the names and places and I don't even know that the story is true. But it could be true!

transport rising from the rapid increase in the number of cars, which have explosive force far outside city boundaries. Villages are suddenly transferred into commuter dormitories. City-centres begin to decay. The whole physical environment changes. You have only to look at the eastern seaboard of America or at Los Angeles to see what can happen here in 10 years' time except that here we have far less room and far more of historic value to destroy.

I would add one more argument in favour of a strong regional focus to British life. This can only be a personal opinion. It is a value judgement and I do not expect to carry everyone with me, because it is based on Christian values which a lot of people today do not accept (though quite what they do accept today, I am not certain). I do not believe that you have a healthy community when it is based on the impersonal and atomised life of a vast city. The Christian is told to love his neighbour as himself and this presupposes that he should try to know who his neighbour is. The Christian Church is based on a mixed community of rich and poor, young and old. It would seem the antithesis of this to have a series of one-class communities. It would also seem wrong to have vast housing estates with no one but young marrieds. The Christian Church is also based on family life and the impersonal world of the bed-sitter in the great city and the lodgings of the 'fly-by-nights' is a far cry from this. A community where a man is known, where reputation and honest dealing count for something, where the community which live together also work together, these would seem to the Christians more conducive to a healthy society. The Kensington bed-sitter may seem to give a glorious freedom from the fussing of provincial parents, but it is a very barren and lonely life and not one I think the human spirit was meant to endure for long.

I am not advocating a return to provincial lace-curtains because the old society had too much of ignorance, super-stition, and intolerance. But there is a happy mean. We were not made to be a featureless dot in a crowd but were made to fit into a place in a community.

What practical conclusions do we draw from all this? First

of all, I think we must say that in having a full-blooded provincial government, with its own Prime Minister, Cabinet and civil service, the North of Ireland is exceptionally fortunate. This may have been an accidental fall-out from the 1922 settlement, but it is one which has served Northern Ireland well. I have little doubt that it has been and still is a tremendous help in the great industrial redevelopment of Northern Ireland. The unemployment ratio in the province is high only because its three major industries were all in decline at the same time. In fact, its record in attracting new industry has been quite outstanding. I have been most impressed too by the way in which the problem of communication with Britain has been tackled. Ulster was far ahead in the development of air freight, of transport in lorry-size containers and in the use of roll-on, roll-off ferries. In looking into these problems for the British Government I have found the Ministry of Commerce far ahead in their detailed knowledge and the information available to shippers. Britain is only now starting to tackle the problem Ulster solved years ago. There is little doubt that the problems of physical and social planning have been dealt with through the provincial government in a way which has not been possible in Britain. Quite what an advantage this is, I do not think anyone can realise until he looks at the problem of doing in Britain the kind of thing which everyone in Ulster takes for granted. Finally, in matters which reflect local, social and religious values, the Northern Ireland Government can reflect the particular needs and wishes of $1\frac{1}{4}$M people far better than a Government trying to find the common denominator in 52 million.

Full provincial government is perhaps needed in a province divided by race and religion and is perhaps not needed where there has been a long history of unity. Critics who point to the continuous rule of one party at Stormont fail to notice that the minority parties are not represented at Westminster and but for Stormont would have no representation at all, except in local government.

Scotland's tradition has been to have a Secretary of State with his own Government Department taking a major part in Scottish affairs. My limited experience in Government service convinces me that there is much more advantage in this than meets the eye. There are only seven Secretaries of State and they have a special position in the Constitution apart from being Cabinet ministers by right of their rank. Scotland is, therefore, represented directly in Cabinet and in all the inter-departmental committees which flow from this. The present Government has created for the first time a Secretary of State for Wales and has thus given it a much better standing as a province than it has had before.

This Government has also given to the newly created Department of Economic Affairs headed by the First Secretary of State the major responsibility for regional affairs and he, in turn, has appointed regional councils and has set up as part of the civil service machine regional planning boards for the North, the North-West, Yorkshire and Humberside, the West and East Midlands, the South-West and South-East and East Anglia. They are, of course, a long way from full regional devolution to a regional government as Ulstermen understand it. They are, for instance, appointed and not elected, but they are also a long step forward from what went before. They have yet to find their feet and make their mark, but from the limited contact I have so far had with them I have no doubt that they will make their mark in due time. Their emphasis and priorities will differ in each region, but already the needs and opportunities of the regions are coming into better focus and the decisions which have to be made bear the imprint of regional needs in a way they have not always done in the past. I am sure that to have a Council and Board is a long step forward towards a balanced industrial development in regions. Companies are not just attracted by money grants, though that helps. What really affects their costs in starting up in a new region is the availability of skilled labour and skilled subcontracting, and speedy communication with customers and suppliers elsewhere. It is meticulous attention to such details as this by the Ministry of Commerce and the whole Northern Ireland Government which has made Ulster so successful in attracting new industry. But this needs regional machinery of government of the kind which the councils and boards are now beginning to provide.

Finally, I am sure that the responsibilities for regions in central Government make it certain that their interests are taken into account when all major decisions which might affect them are taken. However, what is especially important in the machinery of Government is that there shall be centres which can take positive initiatives in regional development and which are also linked to the machinery of Government. My limited experience of Government is that if you want to be in a position to initiate policies—rather than just react to policies initiated by others—then you have to have your place in the Whitehall machine and you have to have a minister who has the political authority to judge and, if satisfied, to promote the policies which are put forward. Otherwise, your ideas are simply part of the extraordinary rag-bag of notions, good, bad, and indifferent which come hurtling in in the post every day in such volume that the good inevitably becomes debased by companionship with the indifferent, not to say bizarre, schemes which are put forward.

But once you are part of the machinery of Government, the leverage which can be given to a well thought out scheme is inevitably quite different. All the problems can be discussed freely and frankly, soundings can be taken from the other interests which would be affected to find their reactions on an informal basis and without commitment and the whole skill of the Government service can be applied to make the scheme workable and acceptable. No individual can do this, nor can any pressure group from outside, but when you are part of the adaptable and very effective machinery of British Government, whatever scheme is workable, sensible and generally acceptable will usually get carried out. I believe, therefore, that the regional councils and planning boards are a long step forward in putting power in Britain in the hands of those most directly concerned with the decisions. The councils are not elected. The boards are still tied to Whitehall and both are democratically accountable, therefore, through Westminster still. Putting twelve or twenty good men and true round a green baize cloth with clean pads of paper does not solve every problem, but it is not for Westminster to propound all the problems and all the solutions. To change the metaphor—it can only put the ball at their feet and I, for one, will be surprised if they do not kick it far and hard, though you would not expect an Ulsterman to tell his fellow Ulstermen, even in Birmingham, that they will do as well as we have done.

CHAPTER THIRTEEN

Britain's Industrial Strength

*This last talk was given in varying forms during a week's tour in the
United States in December 1965 to Americans interested in investment
in Britain. I visited New York, Washington, Boston, Cleveland, and
Detroit and spoke to audiences ranging from the assembled board of the
First National City Bank of New York to a journalists' luncheon at
Cleveland. I also visited a number of companies who were thinking of
investing in Britain. I thought that my view of Britain's economic future
might be treated with some scepticism and was delighted to find that they
all seemed to feel that we had been far too critical of ourselves. (This
is not because they were polite or uncritical. I had to stand up to a lot of
criticism of our Rhodesian policy and explain what I thought would
happen if we took their advice to 'get on or get out'.)*

*The general feeling was that of all American investments around the
world, investment in Britain had been by far the most successful. What
they read about us in the British newspapers gave, they felt, far too
depressing a picture. This view came from both the sophisticated New
York bankers and the tough mid-western production engineers. One of the
latter said to me: 'The trouble with you British is that you don't as the
old song goes "accentuate the positive".' Perhaps this speech which tried
to accentuate the positive is the best on which to end this book.*

The British and American economic positions are both very
similar. Between us we bear the greater part of the world's
burden of overseas investment, aid and defence and although
we both have a surplus on trade visible and invisible, the currency cost of these burdens has drawn down our liquid cash
reserves. In this we are unique. Other countries, including our
close allies, have benefited from the allocation of these burdens
and their immediate cash reserves have increased accordingly.
Both of us, however, have enormous but less liquid overseas

assets. Ours amounts to over $40 billion and yours would, no doubt, come to a bit more. Our immediate cash deficit comes, as yours does, from the help we give to other countries and does not arise any more than yours does from industrial weakness.

It may be useful to compare our economic position with the Common Market countries. The Common Market has attracted a lot more attention than the European Free Trade Area. However EFTA, because it is pragmatic, has perhaps even more of the adaptability needed for survival. It does not depend on political integration, it does not depend on a delicate balance of interests in agriculture. Its members have, for the most part, a long history of democracy and political stability over the centuries which is a good foundation for the association and gives an identity of basic political belief between the partners. Scandinavia, Britain and the two Alpine republics may be a little scattered on the map, but a Briton doing business knows where he is with a Swede or a Swiss because they have all shared the same democratic philosophy for as long as they can remember. With a population of almost 100 million the Association is as big as is needed for all the economies of scale and contains some of the wealthiest countries in Europe. It has survived the temporary surcharge which Britain was forced to impose last year and my own view is that it is and will continue to be one of the strongest economic units in the free world, and a market therefore that we can all depend on. Britain has the added advantage of Commonwealth preference and although this is declining, its absolute volume is very high indeed.

This leads to the effect of the Empire and Commonwealth on Britain's economic position. While it is true that the enormous Empire we ruled until a few years ago gave some benefit to our trading position, it is also true that it took some of our best talent to run it. This is a burden which has been carried by no other country. If you want to judge Britain's innate ability, remember that alone and without fuss we beat the Communist guerillas in the jungles of Malaya. We left India a great and friendly democracy of 400 million people, the largest democracy the world has ever known. Only, now, in the 1960s are we bringing the men who ran this Empire with such skill back to industry. One of the best marketing men I know was a retired General who had been Military Governor of Austria. The former Chief Secretary of Malaya is now personnel director of one of our largest companies. The two best training managers I have known were a naval officer and a colonial district officer. In the last ten years there has been a major re-deployment of our most able people into industry and commerce. The generation which in its twenties won the Battle of Britain and fought with Montgomery in the Western Desert and Normandy is the same generation which, in its forties, is now taking over top jobs in British industry. The new sap is rising in the old British oak.

But what about our actual economic performance over the last few years? Looked at through bankers' eyes, sterling has been exposed and vulnerable in the short term. However, this is fundamentally because we have lent long and borrowed short and not because our manufacturing costs are uncompetitive. We have now taken the most stringent measures on capital account, much tougher than those America has had to take. We have held aid almost level and are committed to a major reduction in our overseas military expenditure. It is also likely that our exports will now grow at a faster rate. For the 1965 National Plan British Industry forecast a $5\frac{1}{4}\%$ rate of annual increase in exports. The forecast of the previous Plan was 3% and was, in the end very accurate. The first year of the current Plan 1965 has been almost exactly as forecast. Over the last few years wage inflation has been far worse in all our major competitor countries, except the United States, than in Britain and since your wages are $2\frac{1}{2}$ times ours, we have a certain amount in hand. ($1·03 for hourly earnings in manufacturing against $2·60 in USA.) Since 1960 your hourly earnings have gone up 15%, ours by 30%. But Japan has gone up by 60%, West Germany by 52%, France by 41% and Italy by 70%. In 1965 all these countries except France have had an appreciably higher increase in hourly earnings than Britain.

Our labour relations will also stand international comparison. In the ten years 1951 to 1961, according to the ILO, we lost

257 days per 1,000 workers, in manufacturing and the other main strike-prone industries (mining, manufacturing, construction and transport). France lost 405, Italy 655 and the United States 1,228. Germany, where there was heavy wage inflation during the period, only lost 81 days per 1,000. However, by 1963, over all employment Germany had lost 66 per 1,000, about the same as the UK's 69·7 and Japan's 57. However, our figures were still far lower than France at 300, Italy at 564 or United States at 1,212.

The British are also prepared to work longer hours than a good many of our neighbours and more prepared to stay at work rather than retire. In Britain the current % of males and females over fifteen and available for work is 61·9, in West Germany 59·3, in France 57·2, in USA (over fourteen) 57·0 and in Italy 53·4. Our average hours worked are 44·8, in West Germany they are 43·3 and USA 40·7.

Britain's industry is not, of course, perfect. Our productivity measured as output per head is much lower than it should be and this is where we have our enormous potential for growth. Since the war we have invested too much overseas and not enough at home. Our investment per head is not nearly so high as America's. Over the last six years our gross fixed capital formation excluding dwellings as a percentage of Gross Domestic Product at factor cost has been between 15% and 16%. In West Germany it has been between 21% and 23%. However, we have now placed strict limits on overseas investment and the Government will shortly come out with proposals for tax incentives for investment which should help to increase the rate of new investment.* This should make a marked difference to our productivity both in giving extra horsepower per worker and in giving greater capacity. For an American company operating in Britain there is also a good deal to be picked up by applying American production practices. I was, until a year ago, managing director of the British Aluminium Company jointly owned by Tube Investments of Birmingham, England, and Reynolds Metals of Richmond, Virginia. The Reynolds output per head was two to three times that in

---

* The scheme of Investment Grants which replaced investment allowances.

Britain. Partly this was due to higher capital investment per head, partly it was due to the average order size being twice as big and partly to skill in the use of labour. We found that American experience in the skilled use of labour made possible great increases in our productivity and we rearranged our marketing and distribution to give us the bigger order sizes necessary for more economic runs. A great many Americans have, in this way, an extremely profitable operation in the UK. I would mention Ford's and Proctor and Gamble as two of the best known because their UK accounts are separately published. Britain has, outside the US, the best industrial infrastructure in the world. The economies of using specialist subcontractors are available as they are available nowhere else. It has a highly skilled labour force. It has its own market of over 50 million and there is a further EFTA market of almost 50 million, making nearly 100 million* in all, which gives it all the potential economies of scale. In its National Economic Plan it has an outline for increasing investment, reducing imports, stepping up exports and increasing the rate of growth of the economy which we are determined to see succeed. If there is a market for a US company in the UK, investment can hardly fail to be profitable.

Most businessmen expect a higher rate of return on overseas investment because they regard it as inherently more risky. As a general proposition I would agree with this. My last company had a third of its investment outside Britain and the international construction company of which I was chief executive before that, had two-thirds overseas. An investor overseas faces the possibility of misunderstanding through differences in languages, difference in custom, differences in labour relations, the possibility of penal taxation, controls, hostility from local interests, hostility from government, exchange risks and even expropriation. In banking slang, his head is on the block for a long time and the rate of return on investment has to be high to justify this risk. However, I am quite certain that investment

* UK 53·4M; Scandinavia (including Finland) 20·4M; Alpine Republics 12·8M; Portugal 9M. Total within the EFTA arrangements 95·6. The more recent arrangements with Eire will bring the eventual free market up to 98·4M.

in Britain is the safest investment an American can make outside his own shores.

Whatever the differences between Britain and the US, the ideological bond between us is far stronger than the bond between either of us and any third country. This is not just a matter of blood being thicker than water. I say this as a matter of observation. I have been engaged in international business for most of my business life. I have also run an Anglo-American company and I know that there are common bonds of basic belief and philosophy which make any Anglo-American partnership better than any other partnership I have known.

There is a remarkable degree of political stability in Britain. We have no Communist party worth the name and no Communists in our Parliament although they have full legal freedom. This can be said of few other major industrial countries in the world.

Investment is not just for today, but for tomorrow and the day after and it is wise to look at the likelihood of further political stability and maturity before making a major investment. I always get a bit annoyed when a salesman tries to sell me something on the grounds that this, that and the other big, wise and shrewd company has bought it. I am tempted to tell him tales of big, wise and shrewd companies which have made terrible mistakes. Nevertheless, the list of American companies who have major investment in Britain is very long and an investor in Britain would, at least, be in good company. Antitrust in the USA does place a final limit on the size of a company's share of US business. But the company's cash flow and expertise may well enable it to pull in extra profits if it goes abroad. In Britain our anti-trust is much more flexible and our criteria for limiting a company's share of the market is not the size of company which is needed for national competition, but the size needed for international competition. Out of 40 possible cases which might have been referred to our Monopolies Commission, in the last year only 2 were actually referred and of these one merger went ahead and the other, which would have given 80% of the market to the merged company did not. The Common Market anti-trust is on the American model. Ours is much more pragmatic and not at all rigid or doctrinaire. I know a bit about both and I would sooner live with ours than with the Sherman Act.

I do not pretend that we can teach American management much that it does not know about production control, about getting the maximum output from the minimum input. There you are the masters and there you can make a real margin of super-profit in a British operation. But very often we are the people who invest what you put into production—the jet aircraft, the hovercraft, the swing-wing are just three very well-known British inventions. The combination of British inventiveness and American application is internationally unbeatable. We also have a good deal more experience in international trading. We export 16% of our gross domestic product against your 4½% and against 10% by the Common Market.* It is no coincidence that many North American subsidiaries in Britain such as Euclid and Massey-Ferguson export as much as 80% of the production of their British subsidiaries. British Ford export about 40% of their production. We have been international traders for centuries, and I think that we can claim to understand the ins and outs of trading around the world as well as any other country. I think also that we have a reputation for fair dealing which is, of course, the basis of international trade and which takes years to build up. In more ways than one a base in Britain, a foreign country which Americans can understand and where they can be understood, can give the key to the markets of the world.

Addendum

What goes for American companies goes also for British and it may be that the advice of this book can be summed up by saying: 'Invest in Britain.'

* See Appendix 1.

Conclusion

Is there a strategy which will pull Britain through the next few years and put us back to the position we held not so long ago as the world's industrial pacemaker? I believe that there is. But I do not think that it depends on our national will alone, or on Government alone, or on management alone, or on labour alone. It requires a national will and it requires that everyone shall make his contribution. When someone says, 'Of course the *real* trouble is . . .', then you know that he is looking to the other side to bail him out.

Of course if the Government threw over all their external commitments at once and we became like Sweden, Germany or Japan, then we would have a lot less trouble. But in real life this is unlikely to happen. External commitments by Britain are too involved with external commitments to Britain. There are genuine worries about the creation of power vacuums. The Foreign Office and the Ministry of Defence have been brought up in a school where you do not take peace for granted.

Of course if unions stopped putting in any pay claims, if employers stopped competing with each other for labour and shop stewards suddenly became quite uninterested in getting more money for those they represent, then, no doubt, our international costs would come down and Government could safely expand the economy without fear of inflation. But the union structure is unlikely to alter overnight and pressure for higher pay has been known to make its contribution to the improvement of productivity.

Of course if all British management were as good as the best we could pay far higher wages and keep the peace of the world to boot, but anyone who has tried to improve the performance of just one company knows that this takes more than a year or two to achieve.

Yet everyone can do something and the cumulative effect

should be more than enough to put us right. Our opportunities are substantial, but our problems are marginal. Our problems matter mainly because they stand in the way of economic development which could be greater and faster than we have even known. We are on a vicious spiral of currency deficits which lead to restrictions on economic growth, which lead to more currency deficits. We need to get on to a virtuous spiral not only for its own sake, not only to solve immediate problems, but also because the virtuous spiral, when we get on to it, is likely to be very virtuous, to lead to far greater economic strength than we have so far dared to imagine. For that reason it is not enough to look for bare solutions, for something which will get us by in fair weather. We need to make quite certain that we succeed. All our policies must give us a margin in hand.

First of all we must look to Government. It is a fact, as I have set out in some detail, that net expenditure on Government account more than explains our balance of payments deficit. On trade, visible and invisible, we have a balance in our favour. In 1965 this was even enough to pay for net overseas investment by business and leave a margin estimated by the Economic Editor of the *Financial Times* at almost £200M (*Financial Times* 23rd June 1966). The same article put the Government Sector deficit at £535M. Making every possible allowance for the off-setting exports, this expenditure far exceeds the overall deficit of £354M. Government military expenditure (net) has risen from £169M in 1960 to £271M in 1965, an increase of 60% in 5 years. Aid has risen from £150M in 1960 to about £200M in 1965, an increase of a third. No one would argue with the proposition that we must do our fair share in the world. It is also arguable that we should, in view of our historic position, do a bit more. But what has happened is that as our real commitments have declined sharply with the independence of our colonial Empire, our net overseas expenditure on Government account has not only not gone down, but has actually increased.

I do not believe that Government military expenditure overseas will in fact go on at this rate. I believe that it will decline as sharply as it has gone up. The 1965 Defence Review was the first step and aimed to save £50M to £100M. Since then the

Indonesian confrontation has come to an end and the Government has started talks with the German Government to end the £90M a year burden of the British forces in Germany.

We do not have to opt out of world affairs, to become a minor state, to cultivate our own back garden. All we have to do is to get the currency spent abroad by the Government back to the kind of level we had in the 1950s. It could be that the balance of trade improved enough to avoid this, but the balance of trade depends on business confidence and it is unrealistic to think that business will be confident when it finds year after year that home demand is held down to deal with a balance of payments deterioration which has nothing to do with trade. I believe that by now Government understands this, but that its public pronouncements will continue to be more cautious than its real intentions. We have in fact been extremely skilful in adjusting our commitments to our resources. I think that in retrospect the early 1960s will be seen as an interim period during which we were temporarily stuck with commitments beyond our resources and that the late 1960s and early 1970s will see commitments and resources come into line again.

Government must not only regulate its own expenditure across the exchanges, it must keep our whole overseas account in some sort of balance. Since the war we have borrowed short and invested long. This is the basis of any banking business and it is the basis of the Sterling Area. At times it seems quite a sensible thing to do. But at other times it looks a good deal more questionable. We have a surplus with the rest of the world on capital account which has been estimated at anything up to £5,000M. But our assets are mostly not in the hands of Government and are not easy to change into cash, whereas our liabilities can be called up in cash from day to day. This puts us in a very vulnerable position and makes us seem far weaker than we really are. It gives the impression that we are living on the benevolence of loans from other countries, whereas in fact other countries have had far more money from us than we have had from them. Almost every major country in the world has had vast infusions of British money to start their economic growth. Yet we have allowed ourselves to get into a technically weak position, because our help to them is long term and, for all practical purposes frozen, whereas their help to us, even though it is much smaller, is to a much greater extent short-term 'hot money'. Since the beginning of 1960 we have invested just short of £2,000M in foreign economies. That amount alone, regardless of Government expenditure abroad, would have been enough to have ended 'stop-go' once and for all. Even during the last two years of economic crisis, private investment overseas amounted to over £700M, enough to pay off a substantial part of the temporary loans we raised to deal with the crisis. The non-trade items on the balance of payments amounted to over £700M in 1964 and over £600M in 1965. That is the handicap which British industry has to set out to overcome in order to achieve a balance of payments surplus. To be £600M to £700M down before you start each year is just too much of a handicap. But looked at the other way round, that is the expenditure on the balance of payments which is within the control of Government and which can therefore be improved by Government policy. I find it very hard to believe that more priority will not be given in the late 1960s to the growth and development of our own economy and I believe that Government overseas expenditure and private investment overseas will be fitted into the needs of the British economy and not the other way round.

There are other policies which Government can pursue which will help, though I do not believe myself that any are so important as those designed to improve the non-trading items on the balance of payments and our international liquidity. If these are successful, as I am sure they will be, given time, then I think that the balance of trade will look after itself. There are, I believe, options open in the field of taxation which will tend to strengthen industry in international competition. If these can be adopted, I think they will have a significant effect. Beyond this I doubt if it is necessary to go. Our interests are served best by creating opportunities for international trade and confidence in international currencies. Confidence is brittle and also important and risks in damaging it are not worth the help they may seem to promise.

Although Government has a vital part to play, the improvement of our strength and standing in the world and of our standard of living must come mainly from the development and growth of British industry. I do not believe that we need be unduly depressed about our industrial performance and potential. A country which can export almost £5,000M every year, 16% of its gross domestic product, 35% of its manufacturing output, cannot be failing. On the other hand I think that our potential for expansion is tremendous—and I use that over-used word advisedly. Other countries, freed from our financial constraints and overseas commitments, have managed a far higher growth rate. American productivity is over twice our productivity. Leaving aside international comparisons, there are tremendous technical improvements in almost every British industry which are waiting to be applied. I believe that the big gains will come from stepping up the rate of investment, from changes in industrial structure, both in the size of companies and the shape of markets, from a major switch from declining to expanding industries and from a much faster rate of technical innovation. Changes will need much more professional and scientifically trained management and more acknowledgement by companies of professional standards. I think that the Economic Development Committees will be a considerable help in bringing about the necessary structural changes and I hope that NEDC will encourage, as it has done in the past, the growth of the institutions necessary to bring about a more professional and scientifically trained management. I am certain too that as the work of the Ministry of Technology develops, it will help to encourage a much faster rate of technical innovation. For all these reasons I shall be most surprised if the rate of productivity does not improve sharply over the next few years.

The unions too can make a further improvement to our industrial strength and standard of living. Whatever the long-term case for a high wages policy on grounds of productivity the next two or three years do demand that the present policy for productivity prices and incomes is given a chance. It may go against the grain and against the experience and training of a union leader to plead for restraint. It may not help him to control the shop floor activist. It may need all the ingenuity and leadership he has got. But in our present financial position it is extremely difficult to have a high rate of growth with money incomes so far ahead of productivity. If incomes cannot be held within the productivity gain by voluntary means (and despite the pending legislation the policy is still voluntary), then there will be the strongest pressure to maintain to the so-called 'classical methods' of deflation and that involves a worse position for everyone in real terms.

Having said all that, those of us who are not trades union officials ought to recognise that theirs is the toughest job of all. Government have the means and power to govern. Management has the means, power and training to improve productivity. But trades unions are voluntary societies with scarcely any sanction except the personal authority of their union leader. Their whole training is to claim higher wages and they can hardly recommend lower wages than managements competing for labour are prepared to concede. While management are busy bidding to attract labour away from each other, the union leader's job is exceptionally difficult. You cannot argue the case for voluntary restraint with union officials, as I have done, without being conscious that they have very real problems. However if they do not succeed, they stand to lose a great deal and for the sake of the authority and standing of the trades union movement, I have no doubt that they will continue to make tremendous efforts to make the policy work.

I think that there will, in addition to the continuing effort to make the voluntary policy work, be a new effort to link wages with productivity. This already happens to some extent at plant level. But I do not see why there should not be an effort to do this at industry level. At plant level all the cards are in the hands of management and they normally make the running. But at industry level, the unions could make a real effort to link wages increases with the productivity level attained by the more advanced companies. It is true that wage claims based on potential productivity would be harder to negotiate than claims based on comparability. But, widely adopted, the system would lead to greater improvements in productivity and to a higher improvement in real terms. It would also make the unions one of the forces which set the pace for the economy and this would be a far better image than that produced by the leapfrogging claims based on comparability, which seem to lead to nothing but wage inflation.

So far I have argued that our problems are technical rather than moral or social. If they are technical, then the right policies ought to produce the right answers and the position is therefore pretty hopeful. If, on the other hand, there are deep-seated moral and social problems, then our position may be much more difficult.

I believe that there is a social problem, but that it is on the way to being put right. I do not believe there is a moral problem which is peculiar to Britain.

To take the social problem first. We have run an Empire with the greatest success for the last ninety years. We have won two major wars and a number of minor ones within living memory. You cannot keep the peace of the world and rule 750 million people without some effect on your institutions and social structure. Adaptable though we are, it is taking us a little time to switch back to being predominantly an industrial power. This is our social problem and I have tried to deal with it in the first chapter and to some extent also in the last. However it is my personal conviction that this problem is well on its way to solution however many vestigial remains there may still be. When Eton College begins to organise visits to nearby factories, something is changing somewhere. Future battles in Europe may well be won on the trading estates of Slough.

The moral problem is more difficult. Over the years there is, I think, a very strong connection between what people believe about the purpose of life and the economic performance of their society. A couple of years ago I wrote a book, *The Christian in Industrial Society* which tried to set out this connection, so far as it could be drawn. But the lessons which have been borne in on us by our elders take a long time to lose their effect and a nation as a whole takes a long time to change its traditional morality. A national crisis may draw out reserves of moral strength or it may cause a complete breakdown and the second world war affected some nations in one way and others in another. It is remarkable, however, how quickly morality has reasserted itself in nations which seemed to have gone over for good to tyranny or paganism.

As one of the small minority of practising Christians I would be the last to deny that a decline in morality matters. Of course it matters—and the form of the ultimate (and inevitable) reaction by society to moral laxity matters perhaps more than the moral laxity itself. A lot of well-meaning people in Germany supported Hitler because they believed that he would clean up the moral laxity of Germany. So at the first he did, in ways much to the point, but he left the world with the feeling that there were worse problems than moral laxity. When the tide does turn, it must be to Christian standards and not to pagan ones, to rationality and not to superstition, to a reasonable course and not to black reaction. As a Christian I look forward more than I can say to the turning of the tide, to the restoration of security and happiness to family life, to the freedom in personal relationships which comes from mutual trust. But whatever the deterioration in small sections of society, I do not yet believe that there has been a deterioration of standards in Britain sufficient to undermine our whole structure of civilised life.

Turning from absolute standards to our standards relative to other countries, I do not believe that Britain can be said to have gone to seed, lost its purpose or its will to work. Maybe, having creamed off our talent into Grammar Schools, those who have been left outside the chosen stream in the educational system have a sense of purposelessness they would not have had before. But every other country with a system of meritocracy has the same problem. America has a far worse problem. Even the Russians have a problem and now, most surprising of all, the Dutch. True we have a problem with gambling and organised crime. But this is nothing to the problems of Chicago and other great American cities. True we are obsessed with sex, but that is a problem of our generation in the Western world and I very much doubt if it is worse in Britain than it is elsewhere. It is certainly worse in some other places than it is in Britain. Every time I come back to this country, I am glad to be home again. I think that we still have a tolerance, a sense of proportion (and the sense of humour which goes with it), a sense of continuity and stability and an undogmatic approach to problems, all of which are a combination rare elsewhere in the world. It is noticeable that those countries with the best economic performance are also those with the longest history of democratic government. Others may catch up for a time, but sustained progress seems to be linked to a democratic way of life, to the achievement of a consensus in society. However sharp our immediate conflicts may seem to be, they never seem even remotely to threaten the cohesion of society as they have done so often elsewhere. While we have this cohesion, I believe that we still have a solid base on which to build a strong and prosperous society.

Appendix 1

INTERNATIONAL COMPARISONS ON EXPORTS

Exports as % of Gross Domestic Product	1959	1960	1961	1962	1963	1964
UK	16·2	16·5	16·0	15·9	16·2	15·5
EEC (excluding intra- EEC trade)	12·0	12·1	11·5	10·5	10·1	10·4
W Germany (excluding exports to EEC) ..	13·8	13·2	12·4	11·4	11·2	—
UK (excluding exports to EFTA	14·0	13·9	13·4	13·2	13·5	—
USA	4·0	4·5	4·5	4·3	4·4	4·5
Japan	11·4	11·2	9·7	10·0	9·7	—

		1964	$ 1000M.	
	USA	EEC Total	EEC net of intra-trade	UK
Exports	26·1	42·6	24·2	12·3
GDP at factor cost ..	576·8	233·5	233·5	79·8
Exports as % of GDP	4·5	18·2	10·4	15·5

To arrive at the fairest comparison of performance it is, I think right to exclude trade within a community. One would not count sales from New Jersey to Alabama as an American export. Most of the manufacturing output of the small EEC countries like Holland and Belgium is, theoretically, exported, but a sale from Antwerp to Rotterdam or from Amsterdam to Dusseldorf or vice-versa is not quite the same thing as a sale from Birmingham to Tokyo. Strictly one should take EFTA sales out of Britain's performance and I have given a percentage on this basis. But the EEC has a common external tariff against all strangers and EFTA does not. Britain's tariff advantage over EEC in selling to Scandinavia is often only a matter of 2%. But Germany's advantage over Britain in selling to Italy or France is more likely to be 10% to 15%.

Appendix 2

DEFENCE

£M

	1960	1961	1962	1963	1964	1965
Net (including Military Grants	169	192	225	233	263	271

[*Source:* Cmnd. 2966, Table 14.]

AID

	1960	1961	1962	1963	1964	1965
UK Government Economic Aid	150	162	150	158	191	n.a. [but about 200].

[*Source:* UK Balance of Payments 1965, Table 27.]

PRIVATE INVESTMENT

Successive British Governments have also taken credit for UK *private investment* in developing countries as a reinforcement of Government aid and have argued internationally that such investment should be added to the amount of official aid to reflect the real contribution by the UK to developing countries.

Appendix 2

The figures for private investment in *developing countries** have been:

	1960	1961	1962	1963	1964	1965
Private Investment (including Oil)	143	124	68	61	75	n.a.

[*Source:* as above, Table 28.]

NET OVERSEAS INVESTMENT

These figures show the balance of all private investment trans-actions by the UK and by foreigners in the UK.

The main figures are:

Increase in assets —
Increase in liabilities +

	1960	1961	1962	1963	1964	1965
By UK†	−316	−304	−236	−335	−399	−312
In UK	+233	+426	+247	+278	+152	+175
Total Private Investment *net*	−83	+122	+11	−57	−247	−137

[*Source:* Cmnd. 2966, Table 18.]

TOTAL OF DEFENCE, AID, OVERSEAS INVESTMENT

On the basis of the above figures, the overall position for these "Invisibles" is as follows

	1960	1961	1962	1963	1964	1965
Net	402	232	364	448	701	608

* The 'developed' Commonwealth countries – Australia, N.Z. and Canada – are excluded.

† These figures are net of portfolio disinvestment. In 1965 this amounted to £90M so that new private direct investment was £402M. This was largely due to the Government's 1965 measures which brought back to the reserve 25% of the gross sales of non-sterling securities.

216

Index

A

Accountancy profession, 27, 92–8, 100–3
ICA lectures and courses, 103
Aid and investment in developing
countries, 176–7, 198, 199, 215–16
Alpine Republic, 201
Aluminium industry, 61–4, 67
Amalgamated Engineering Union, 187
Anatomy of Britain (Anthony Sampson),
56
Anti-trust laws, *see under* United States
Appelby, Robert, 159
Asquith, H. H. (Earl of Oxford), 20
Association of Certified Accountants,
102
A T & T, 111
Australia, 190, 216
Austria (Austria-Hungary), 188–9

B

Balance Group (Cambridge University), 17, 30
speech to, 18–30
Balance of Payments, 23, 24, 123, 127,
128, 134, 136, 167, 170, 173, 215
exports, annual value of, 135, 141,
208
Bar Council, 28
Beatles, the, 121
Beeby, G. N., 159
Belfast, talk to accountants at (1965),
92–104, 191
Belfast Telegraph, 183
Belgium, 138
Birmingham, talk to Ulster Societies at
(1965), 183–96
BNEC, 126, 127
Board of Trade, investment grants and,
132

Boarding schools, 20–1, 24
public school spirit, 22
Bolton, J. E., 159
Bristol, BIM branch at, 105
Bristol Chamber of Commerce, speech
to (1965), 162–171
British Aluminium Company, 58, 101,
200
British Chemical Contractors Association, 156
British Institute of Management, talks
to (1965), 47–57, 80–91, 105–16
British Medical Journal, 38
British Rail, 155
Business economists, 95–6, 99
Business schools, 30, 33, 38–9, 50, 58,
138

C

Caldecote, Lord, 154, 159
Cambrai, battle of, 35
Cambridge, Social Accounting Matrix,
122, 149
Cambridge University, 17, 30
Appointments Board (Annual
Report), 18
Campbell, Lord, 159
Canada, 190, 216
Capital cities and provincial capitals,
187–91
Capital-Earnings ratios, 76–7
Carnaby Street, 121
CBI Journal, 122
Central Electricity Generating Board,
157
Chartered Accountants, *see under*
Accountancy profession *and* Institute of
Chartered Company, the, 105

Index

Index

European Free Trade Area, 62, 112, 213–14
  strength of, 198, 201
Export Corporations, 126, 141, 157
Exports:
  EDC for, 154–5, 157, 159
  expansion and growth potential, 200, 208
  international comparisons, 213–14
  percentage of gross domestic product, 213
  volume and value of, 135, 141, 174–6, 208
    to Europe, 155

F

Federal systems (of government), 189–190
Federation of British Industries, 166
Finance Act (1965), 24
Financial Times, 205
Finland, 201
First National City Bank, 197
Fords (of Britain), 201, 203
Foreign Office, 204
Fortune, list of major companies, 136
Fox, Alan, 37
France, 199, 214
  strike losses (1951–61), 200
Franz Joseph, Emperor, 189

G

Gallipoli campaign, 35
General Agreement on Trade and Tariffs, 174
General Electric Company, 111
General Motors, 111
Germany, Federal Republic of, 29, 109, 124, 136, 190, 199, 204, 213, 214
  Rhine Army costs, 119, 206
Glasgow, branch of CBI, 117
'Good company, the', philosophy and practices of, 113–15

Government expenditure, 205–6, 207
Goyder, George, 105
Grooms Coffee House, 28
Gross Domestic Product, 200, 203, 208, 213
Guinness, Sir Alec, 64

H

Harland and Wolff, 188
Harvard business school, 50
Hilton Hotel, New York, 70
Hitler, Adolf, 211
Holland, 136, 138
Hungary (Austria-Hungary), 188–9

I

Imperial Chemical Industries, 136
Imperial College, 20
Imperial England, 19–20, 21–2
Imports, 141–2, 181
  EDC study on, 155
Incomes policy, *see* Prices and Incomes
India, 20, 198
Indian civil service, 20
Industrial Reorganisation Corporation, 13, 117, 130, 136–8
Inflation (in other countries), 124
Inland Revenue:
  depreciation allowances, 94
  Investment Grants, 94, 117, 130–6, 200
Institute of Builders, 139
Institute of Chartered Accountants, 93, 102–4
  courses and lectures by, 103
Institute of Industrial Administration, 53
  Professional Standards Committee, 53
Institute of Municipal Treasurers, 102
International Business Machines, 111
International Labour Office, 199

Index

International Management Congress
(1963), 70
talk at, 71–9
Investment grants, 94, 117, 130–6, 200
Investors Chronicle, 163
IRC, *see* Industrial Reorganisation
Corporation
Isle, Mosley, 159
Israel, 127
Italy, 199, 214
strike losses (1951–61), 200

J

James Dunn Lecture (Newcastle
University), 31–46
James of Rusholme, Lord, 67
Japan, 136, 199, 204, 213
strike losses (1951–61), 200

K

Kennedy Round, the, 174

L

Labour:
hoarding of, 151
mobility of, 167, 171
regional imbalance, 167
relations, international comparisons,
199–200
Lancet, The, 38
Latham, Sir Joseph, 159
Law Courts, 28
Laws Stores, Gateshead, 32
Leicester Branch, BIM, 80
'Little Neddies', *see* Economic Develop-
ment Committees
Lloyd, Selwyn, 62, 162
London, pull of the metropolis, 187–8

London Graduate School of Business
Studies, 139
Lords, House of:
attendance fee, 88
Official Report, 158
Lough Neagh, 184

M

McClelland, Arthur, 32, 33
McClelland, Grigor, 32
Macmillan, Harold, 162
Maginot Line, 89
Malaysia (Malaya)), 198
reduction of forces in, 119, 125
Man in the White Suit, film, 64
Management consultants and selection,
89–90, 93, 97–8, 103, 153
Management Consultants Association,
103
Management Selection, 68
Management Studies, Journal of, 58
Managerial Economics (Joel Dean), 63
Manchester Business School, 32
Massey-Ferguson, 203
Mathys, H. R., 159
Maudling, Reginald, 162
Merchant banks, 85
Metternich, 189
Mills, C. Wright, 51
Milton Story, The (Alan Fox), 37
MIT business school, 50
Mitchell, Sir Stewart, 159
Monopolies Commission, 29, 202
Montgomery, Viscount, 199
Moyola river, 184

N

National Economic Development
Council ('Neddy'), 13, 24, 29, 50,
97, 122, 145, 146, 151, 155
Imported Manufactures paper, 155
NEDO, 148, 150, 151, 208

Index

National Economic Plan (1965), 27, 51,
117–38, 144, 148, 150, 151 (1963),
152, 199, 200, 201
National Incomes Commission, 169
NEDDY, *see* National Economic Development Council
NEDO, 148, 150, 151
Negotiation (the Negotiator), 45–6
NEP, *see* National Economic Plan
Nevinson, H. W., 21
New York, International Management
Congress at, 70
New Zealand, 216
Newcastle University, 31
Nicholson, David, 159
Northern Ireland, *see* Ulster

Price, Waterhouse, 77
Prices and Incomes:
National Board for, 13, 162
policy, 118, 127
effect on productivity and living
costs of, 15
speeches on, 162–82
Prices and Incomes Bill, 118, 119
Procter and Gamble, 201
Productivity:
factory forums, 182
output per head, 200
speeches on, 160–82
trade unions and, 178–9, 181, 208–9
Professional bodies, 26, 27, 28
Royal Charters, 27
Public school spirit, 22
Punch magazine, 19, 30

O

OECD, 160
Old Boy Network, 54–5
Operational researchers, 100, 102
Organisation Man (William Whyte), 43
Overseas investments and assets, 119,
123, 173–4, 201, 207, 215
Oxford and Henley Staff College, 32
Oxford University, 30
Business Summer School, address to,
58–69

Q

Qualifications, management code of
ethics, 53–4
Queen's Award (for exports), 115

R

Resale price maintenance, 29
Responsible Company, The (George Goyder), 105
Restrictive Trade Practices Act, 29
Reynolds Metal, 200
Rhine Army, costs of, 119, 206
Rhodesian crisis, 125
Robinson, Sir Leslie, 159
Robinson–Patman Act, 29, 110, 111
Robson, Sir Thomas, 159
Rochester, Assembly Rooms, 47
Rolling Stones, the, 121
Rolls-Royce, 188
Rootes strike, 35
Royal Charters, 27
Royal Commissions, 153
Runge, Sir Peter, 166
Russia, corporation state philosophy,
110

P

Parkinson's Law, 51
Parsons and Reyrolle, 188
Passchendaele, battle of, 35
Pax Americana, 17
Pax Britannica, 17, 22
Peru, 186–7
'Plan, The', *see* National Economic
Plan
Plowden Committee, on aircraft industry, 158
Portugal, 201
Power, Ministry of, 157
Powers-Samas machine, 32–3

Index

S

Sampson, Anthony, 56
Scandinavia, 29, 62, 155, 201, 214
Schlieffen Plan, 89
Scotland, 193–4
Selective Employment Tax, 135
Shell Company, 136, 187
Sherman Acts, 110, 111, 203
Shipping strike, 118, 119
Shrewsbury School, 21
Slough Trading Estate, 25, 210
Slump (of 1929/31), 167
Social Accounting Matrix, Cambridge, 122, 149
Somme, battle of, 20, 35
Standard Oil, 82
Standardisation of products, 142, 143
Stanford business school, 50
Sterling Area, 206
Stokes, Sir Donald, 159
Stormont, 193
Strike losses (1951–61), international comparisons, 200
Suez Canal, 20
    1956 crisis, 21, 22
Sunbury-on-Thames, 186
Swallow, William, 159
Sweden, 124, 138, 204
Switzerland, 29, 136, 138, 190–1

T

Technology, Ministry of, 13, 14, 24, 208
Times, The, 13, 183
Trade unions:
    difficulties of leadership in current conditions, 209
    EDCs and, 181
    productivity and, 178–80, 208–9
Trades Union Congress, 145
    speech to research officers, 171–82
Transport & General Workers Union, 187
Trevelyan–Northcote civil service reforms, 20
Tube Investments, 200

U

Ulster, 185, 193, 194, 196
    Ministry of Commerce, 193, 194
Ulster Societies, talk at Birmingham (1965), 183–96
Unilever, 28, 136
United States, 18, 21, 23, 50–1, 123, 136–7, 140, 213
    anti-trust laws, 29, 106, 110, 111, 112, 168, 190, 202
    British embassy in, 127
    business schools, 5, 38
    gross domestic product, 176
    investment in Britain, 202–3
    lecture tour talk (1965), 197–203
    productivity in, 208
    strike losses (1951–61), 200
    wages and incomes, 169, 172, 177, 199
University Grants Committee, report on 'First Employment of University Graduates', 18
Utilisation, full, of plant and machines, 142

V

Vickers, Tower, 187
Victoria, Queen, 190
Victorian England, 19–20, 21

W

Wage freeze (1962), 162
Wales, Secretary of State for, 194
Washington, British embassy in, 127
Waterloo, battle of, analogy, 151
Webb–Pomerene Act, 110
Weeks, Sir Hugh, 159
Wellington College, 20
Westinghouse, 111
White Collar (C. Wright-Mills), 51
Whyte, William, 43, 51
World Bank, 70